ARCHANGELS
101

❧ ALSO BY DOREEN VIRTUE ❧

Books/Kits/Oracle Board

Audio/CD Programs

Angel Therapy® *Meditations*
Fairies 101 (abridged audio book)
Goddesses & Angels (abridged audio book)
Angel Medicine (available as both 1- and 2-CD sets)
Angels among Us (with Michael Toms)
Messages from Your Angels (abridged audio book)
Past-Life Regression with the Angels
Divine Prescriptions
The Romance Angels
Connecting with Your Angels
Manifesting with the Angels
Karma Releasing
Healing Your Appetite, Healing Your Life
Healing with the Angels
Divine Guidance
Chakra Clearing

DVD Program

How to Give an Angel Card Reading

Oracle Cards (44 or 45 divination cards and guidebook)

Archangel Raphael Healing Oracle Cards
Archangel Michael Oracle Cards
Angel Therapy® *Oracle Cards*
Magical Messages from the Fairies Oracle Cards
Ascended Masters Oracle Cards
Daily Guidance from Your Angels Oracle Cards
Saints & Angels Oracle Cards
Magical Unicorns Oracle Cards
Goddess Guidance Oracle Cards
Archangel Oracle Cards
Magical Mermaids and Dolphins Oracle Cards
Messages from Your Angels Oracle Cards
Healing with the Fairies Oracle Cards
Healing with the Angels Oracle Cards

All of the above are available at your local
bookstore, or may be ordered by visiting:

Hay House USA: **www.hayhouse.com**®
Hay House Australia: **www.hayhouse.com.au**
Hay House UK: **www.hayhouse.co.uk**
Hay House South Africa: **www.hayhouse.co.za**
Hay House India: **www.hayhouseco.in**

Doreen's Website: **www.AngelTherapy.com**

ARCHANGELS
101

How to Connect Closely with Archangels
Michael, Raphael, Gabriel, Uriel, and
Others for Healing, Protection, and Guidance

DOREEN VIRTUE

HAY HOUSE, INC.
Carlsbad, California • New York City
London • Sydney • Johannesburg
Vancouver • Hong Kong • New Delhi

Copyright © 2010 by Doreen Virtue

Published and distributed in the United States by: Hay House, Inc.: www
.hayhouse.com • *Published and distributed in Australia by:* Hay House
Australia Pty. Ltd.: www.hayhouse.com.au • *Published and distributed
in the United Kingdom by:* Hay House UK, Ltd.: www.hayhouse.co.uk
• *Published and distributed in the Republic of South Africa by:* Hay
House SA (Pty), Ltd.: www.hayhouse.co.za • *Distributed in Canada
by:* Raincoast: www.raincoast.com • *Published in India by:* Hay House
Publishers India: www.hayhouse.co.in

Editorial supervision: Jill Kramer • *Project editor:* Alex Freemon
Design: Tricia Breidenthal

Library of Congress Cataloging-in-Publication Data

Virtue, Doreen.
  Archangels 101 : how to connect closely with archangels Michael, Ra-
phael, Gabriel, Uriel, and others for healing, protection, and guidance /
Doreen Virtue. -- 1st ed.
      p. cm.
  ISBN 978-1-4019-2638-0 (hardcover : alk. paper) 1. Archangels--Miscel-
lanea. 2. Spiritual life. I. Title.
  BF1999.V5855 2010
  202'.15--dc22
                                                2010005085

Hardcover ISBN: 978-1-4019-2638-0
Digital ISBN: 978-1-4019-2936-7

14 13 12 11   5 4 3 2
1st edition, October 2010
2nd edition, January 2011

Printed in China

To God.
Thank You for
the beloved archangels.

CONTENTS

WHO ARE THE
ARCHANGELS?

The word *archangel* is derived from the Greek *archi*, which means "first, principal, or chief"; and *angelos,* which means "messenger of God." So, archangels are the chief messengers of God.

Archangels are extremely powerful celestial beings. Each has a specialty and represents an aspect of God. You can think of archangels as facets on the face of God, the ultimate jewel and gem of the universe. These facets, or archangels, are prisms that radiate Divine light and love in specific ways to everyone on Earth.

The archangels are one of God's original creations, and they existed long before humankind or organized religions. They belong to God, not to any

specific theology. Therefore, archangels work with people of all different beliefs and paths. In fact, they work with anyone who asks.

Artwork portrays archangels as ideal human forms with large eagle- or swanlike wings, in contrast to artistic depictions of cherubs as babies with small wings.

In this book, I'll discuss 15 of God's archangels from the monotheistic tradition, including the famous angels of the Bible and noncanonical books (the Dead Sea Scrolls). I've only included the angels recognized by Judeo-Christian theologians.

My research comes from:

- The traditional canonical Judeo-Christian Bible (either the New International or the King James version)

- The apocryphal books (those that were not included in the traditional or canonical Bible, but which are still considered sacred writings) such as the Book of Enoch (which was first written in Ethiopian and later in Hebrew) and the Book of Esdras

- The mystical Jewish Kabbalah (which recognizes archangels as guardians of the spiritual pathway or Tree of Life), including the Zohar

- The monotheistic Qu'ran

- The teachings of the Eastern Orthodox Church

I've combined these scriptural references with knowledge acquired from my own years of working with and teaching about these archangels. As you'll discover, each archangel chapter includes a true story or two to illustrate how archangels are involved with our modern lives, as well as prayers scattered throughout that relate to the particular archangel's specialties.

The Nine Choirs of Angels

Angelology, the study of angels, holds that there are nine "choirs" or branches of angels, which include:

- **Seraphim:** These are the highest order of angels, said to be shining bright, as they are closest to God. They are pure light.

- **Cherubim:** Usually portrayed as chubby children with wings à la Cupid, the Cherubim are the second-highest order. They are pure love.

- **Thrones:** The triad of Seraphim, Cherubim, and Thrones resides in the highest realms of Heaven. Thrones are the bridge between the material and the spiritual, and represent God's fairness and justice.

- **Dominions:** The Dominions are the highest in the next triad level of angels. They are the overseers or managers of angels, according to God's will.

- **Virtues:** These angels govern the order of the physical universe, watching over the sun, moon, stars, and all of the planets, including Earth.

- **Powers:** As their name implies, this choir comprises peaceful warriors who purify the universe from lower energies.

- **Principalities:** The third triad consists of the angels closest to Earth. The Principalities watch over the planet, including nations and cities, to ensure God's will of peace on Earth.

- **Archangels:** These are the overseers of humankind and the guardian angels. Each archangel has a speciality representing an aspect of God.

- **Guardian angels:** You, and every individual, have personal guardian angels assigned to you throughout your life.

This model of nine choirs was derived from the biblical references to Seraphim and Cherubim, which were expanded upon in the 5th-century theologian Pseudo-Dionysius's writings and then popularized in John Milton's poetic work *Paradise Lost*.

Interacting with Archangels

Since archangels are so close to Earth and humankind, it's natural for us to connect with them. In fact, the Bible is filled with accounts of people interacting with Michael and Gabriel. The archangels still interact with us in conjunction with God's will of peace.

We don't pray to archangels, nor do we worship them. All glory goes to God. We work with archangels simply because they are God's intended gift to us all, and part of the Divine plan for peace.

So why don't we simply direct all questions and requests to God? Because the archangels are extensions of God who are easier to hear and feel during times of great stress. Their vibrations are very condensed, and they're palpable and practically tangible. Just as looking at a sunset or a rainbow reminds us of God's love, so do the archangels.

You don't need to be saintly or a perfectly behaved person to elicit the archangels' help. They look past human mistakes and see the inner goodness within us all. They want to bring peace to Earth by helping us all be *peaceful*. So their mission includes helping the *un*peaceful people of the world.

As holograms of God's omnipresence, the archangels are unlimited beings. Remember the promise

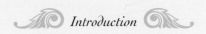

that Jesus made: "I am with you always"? Well, the archangels—like Jesus—are able to be with each person who calls upon them.

The key is that the archangels will never violate your free will by intervening without permission, even if to do so would make you happier. They must wait until you give permission in some way: a prayer, a cry for help, a wish, a visualization, an affirmation, or a thought. The archangels don't care *how* you ask for their help, but only that you *do*.

You also needn't worry about asking for the archangels' help incorrectly. You don't have to be specially trained or use fancy invocations to garner their attention. Any sincere call for aid is enough, as all they require is your permission.

Affirmative and supplicant prayers work. In the former, it's a positive here-and-now statement or visualization, such as "Thank you, Archangel Michael, for protecting me"; and in the latter, it's an appeal, like "Please protect, Archangel Michael." Both yield the same results.

This is also the answer when asking, "Should I call upon God directly? Should I ask God to send the appropriate angels? Or should I call upon the angels directly?" These questions imply that there's a separation between God and the angels, and there is not.

This book will help you get to know the specialties, characteristics, personalities, and energies of my favorite archangels. In this way, you'll develop a closer relationship with them. The more you work with them, the more you'll begin to trust them. You'll feel peaceful, knowing for certain that you're safe and protected in all situations.

The Archangels in Sacred Texts

The archangels have been described in spiritual texts such as:

— **The Bible:** Michael and Gabriel are the only two archangels specifically named in the Bible. The Book of Daniel describes both angels, including Gabriel's role in helping Daniel interpret his visions, and a mention of Michael as "one of the chief princes." In Luke, Gabriel appears in the famous "Behold, I bring you good tidings of great joy" annunciation of the forthcoming births of John the Baptist and Jesus Christ. Michael also appears in the Book of Jude, to protect Moses's body, and in Revelations.

— **Apocryphal and Talmudic biblical books:** The scriptural texts that aren't in the canonical Bible

are still regarded as sacred, and are part of the Bible of the Eastern Orthodox and other churches. The Book of Enoch discusses the archangels Michael, Raguel, Gabriel, Uriel, and Metatron. The Book of Tobit is the account of Archangel Raphael guiding Tobias in his travels and helping him create healing ointments for his father, Tobit. The second book of Esdras (recognized by the Coptic church) refers to Archangel Uriel, calling him the "angel of salvation."

— **The Qur'an:** The Islamic scripture was revealed to Muhammad by the archangel Gabriel (Jibrayil). The Qur'an and Muslim traditions also describe archangels Michael (Mikaaiyl), Raphael (Israfel), and Azrael (Izrael).

How Many Archangels Are There?

The answer depends upon whom you ask.

Traditionally, people think of the quartet of Michael, Raphael, Gabriel, and Uriel. However, as I mentioned, only two are named in the traditional Bible. Muslims hold that there are four archangels: Gabriel, Michael, Azrael, and Raphael.

The Bible's Book of Revelation tells us that there are seven archangels, and in the noncanonical Book of Tobit, Raphael says he is one of seven. The Gnostics also held seven archangels in esteem. Historians believe that the number seven comes from the Babylonians' blend of religion and astronomy, with reverence for the seven planets' mystical powers.

Which seven archangels make this list, though, differs from source to source. And that's not even taking into account that each archangel's name has alternative spellings and pronunciations.

In the Judaic mystical Kabbalah, ten archangels represent each of the *Sephiroth*, or aspects of God. Metatron is the chief archangel in this tradition.

So the topic of how many archangels exist can be confusing and subjective. I tried to answer this question to my own satisfaction while researching and writing my book *Archangels & Ascended Masters*. My methodology was to learn as much as I could about the archangels, and then have personal interactions and connections with each one. The 15 archangels whom I was easily able to reach and research, and who emanated God's pure love and light, were included in that book—and in this one.

In truth, there are legions of archangels helping us here on Earth. In fact, Eastern Orthodox theology holds that there are thousands. My prayer is that

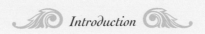

we will be open-minded, and welcome trustworthy archangels into our sphere of spiritual friends.

If you're concerned about lower energies, I want to reassure you that there's no way that any fear-based physical or spiritual being could mimic the profound healing love and light that emanate from our beloved archangels of God. Plus, if you ask God, Jesus, and Archangel Michael to shield you from lower energies, they're happy to ensure that only beings of light are with you.

Yes, there *are* lower-energy, fear-based spiritual beings whom some call "angels" but who are actually Earthbound spirits. For example, an "archangel" named Samael was once called the "Angel of Light" or the "Lightbearer." But then Samael's light fell, and he became vengeful and dark. This seems to be the basis of the ideology about Lucifer, which isn't specifically mentioned in the Bible but is discussed through mythology and legend.

In this book, I've stayed far away from these dark "angels" of occultists, including those that are supposedly associated with King Solomon. The occult legend holds that Solomon used his magical ring embossed with the Star of David to control demons who built his Temple. These 72 demons are sometimes presented as a list of angel names, but they're not angels. These so-called Solomonic Lesser and Greater Keys teachings bring in dark and untrustworthy energy. (By the way, I don't believe that the good King Solomon worked with lower energies.)

Some occultists invoke the names of the sacred archangels Michael, Raphael, Gabriel, and Uriel in fear-based ceremonies. My advice: Stay away from any religion or spiritual practice that is fear or guilt based. Stick with the real angels of God's light and love—they're the ones who will really bring you the peace and happiness you desire.

The main response I hear from those who begin working with archangels is: "They changed my life for the better!" People become happier, healthier, and more peaceful and sure-footed as a result of calling upon them. The archangels are a very personal way to connect with God's love and wisdom.

May each moment of your day be carried upon the wings of angels!

— **Doreen Virtue**

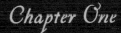

Chapter One

MICHAEL

*"Dear Archangel Michael, thank you for
protecting me and my loved ones. Thank you
for watching over us, our homes, and our vehicles.
Thank you for giving me the courage and confidence
to move forward with my Divine life purpose."*

Michael is also known as: Saint Michael, Mikael, Miguel, Mika'il, Mikha'el, Beshter, or Sabbathiel

Michael's name means: "He who is like God"

Michael is probably the most famous of all the archangels. He's been sainted, churches are named for him, he features prominently in the Bible and other sacred texts, and countless men are named after him.

Ancient and modern artwork portray Michael as a muscular, athletic archangel with intensely powerful facial expressions and body language. Usually he's painted with his sword poised above a pinned-down demon. This is to signify Michael's primary purpose of slaying the ego and fear.

His sword is actually made of light instead of metal, and is used to detach us from the grips of fear. Michael knows that if we aren't afraid, we're at peace.

Some believe that Michael and Jesus are the same Divine son of God because they have such similar missions. I've found that the two work very closely together yet still maintain distinct personas. In my historical psychic research, I found evidence of Jesus and Michael working together, as Earth was originally populated by humans. They've always been here on Earth, and they always will be . . . protecting all of us as well as the planet.

Michael is one of the two archangels named in the canonical Bible (along with Gabriel). In the Book of Daniel, Michael identifies himself to the prophet Daniel as the protector of Israel. Michael protected Moses's body in Jude, and fought dragons (the historical symbol of evil or the ego) in Revelations. In the apocryphal Book of Enoch, Michael is called the "prince of Israel," who teaches and protects the prophet Enoch.

Jewish tradition holds that Michael appeared to Abraham, was likely the angel who helped Moses receive the Ten Commandments tablets, and intervened to save the lives of Isaac and Jacob.

Catholicism teaches that Michael will defeat the Antichrist in the end times. Because of his miraculous interventions, Catholic tradition reveres Michael and has named him the patron saint of police officers and other rescue workers.

Michael is also a patron saint of the sick, and is traditionally seen as a great healer. He is often invoked along with Jesus, Raphael, and other saints associated with healing physical maladies.

Each archangel has a speciality; and some, like Michael, have several. His include the following:

Protection

As the defender of all that is pure, Michael is the epitome of strength and valor. He intervenes miraculously to save lives and to protect our bodies, loved ones, vehicles, belongings, and reputations.

An Air Force officer named Earl T. Martin is alive today because he heard and followed Michael's verbal warning.

Earl was in Alaska at an Air Force camp. As he lay down in his pup tent for a rest, he heard a clear male voice tell him, "Do not lie down facing this position in the tent. Face in the completely opposite direction immediately, and do not hesitate."

Earl followed Michael's directive and reversed his position. A moment later, he heard gunfire and felt a sting on his ankle. One of the military personnel had accidentally fired his rifle and grazed Earl's ankle. If Earl hadn't heeded Michael's warning, the bullet would have hit his head!

Protection While in Vehicles

"Thank you, Archangel Michael, for protecting my vehicle and everyone in it, as well as everyone driving and walking around us."

I've read and been told many accounts of Michael saving a driver from a potential accident, as in Hilda Blair's story.

Every morning Hilda asks Archangel Michael to protect her, especially while she's driving. And on a recent morning, she witnessed the results of her prayers and Michael's protection.

Hilda was driving her small car on a fast-moving highway. A large white truck in front of her started to move into the lane to the left. So Hilda decided to speed up and take the space it had occupied. Just as she was about to do so, though, Hilda heard a voice say, "Stay where you are. Do not move forward. He is going to change his mind." Hilda's first thought was that this voice was wrong, as she watched the white truck moving into the left lane.

But then the truck swerved back in front of Hilda's car. If she had sped up, it would have hit her! She thanked Michael for his protection, and was relieved that she'd heeded his guidance.

Hilda's and Earl's stories illustrate Michael's method of protecting us by delivering to-the-point guidance that we perceive as a disembodied male voice. He only tells us as much as we need to hear, such as "Change lanes right now." If you hear this voice, follow its instructions.

When you climb into a car, it's important to ask Michael for protection, as Hilda did. Remember that the archangels can only intervene if you ask for their help.

Another woman, named Suzie O'Neill, also found that her life was saved by asking for Michael's protection before she began driving.

Suzie and her daughter were on a California highway when she noticed a car sliding sideways ahead of them. Time seemed to slow down as Suzie watched the bumper head straight toward her sports car. Then, miraculously, the other car stopped sliding and a crash was avoided.

Suzie's daughter, a skeptic about angels and miracles, asked, "Did you see that?" But Suzie knew what had happened, as she'd asked for Archangel Michael's protection right before they got into the car that day. So when they stopped and a man walked up to see if they were okay—and then vanished without a trace—Suzie knew that it was one more way in which Michael was watching over them.

Most likely, Suzie's daughter is no longer skeptical about the angels' miraculous powers and means of protection. Those of us who have had an angel experience shift from merely *believing* to without-a-doubt *knowing* in the instant that it takes Michael to save our lives.

If you forget to call upon Michael prior to getting in a car (or any other form of transportation), you can elicit his help instantly during a crisis. I admire people like Amanda Peart in the following story, who had the wherewithal to call upon Michael in an emergency situation, when most people would have simply screamed or let loose with expletives.

When a man in a little blue car almost veered into Amanda's vehicle, she was startled. Then he

started yelling at Amanda and swerved repeatedly. She soon realized that the man was acting out "road rage," and that she was in danger of being coerced into an accident. She says, "There was a great deal of traffic, and I was sure he was going to kill me."

As soon as she realized the danger she was in, Amanda called for Archangel Michael's protection. Suddenly a white van appeared beside her, literally from nowhere. It pulled in front of Amanda and got between her car and the blue one. It stayed there, blocking the other car from her. Finally, the blue car pulled off the freeway. Still, the van stayed with Amanda until she nearly reached her home.

That white van was an angel, and I've read similar accounts where a mysterious vehicle (usually angelic white) shows up to protect, or shine light, during frightening driving situations. Many Archangel Michael stories involve vehicles such as ambulances and buses, which miraculously appear in time to help someone . . . and then disappear afterward.

Archangel Michael can protect you anytime you step into a car, boat, airplane, or train. All you have to do is ask.

Protection of Belongings

*"Dear Archangel Michael, please safeguard
my home and all of my possessions,
helping me feel safe and secure."*

The angels protect our possessions to help maintain our peace of mind. They are aware of the stress that stems from insecurity about our personal items, so they happily watch over these things for us. After all, the angels are unlimited beings, so protecting our belongings doesn't take them away from other vital missions.

Since Archangel Michael is the chief protector of everyone, it makes sense that he's involved with watching out for our possessions. (Again, this role doesn't take him away from more pressing matters, since Michael is omnipresent.) Here is a case in point:

As she rode in a rental-car shuttle van, Carmen Carignan was horrified to realize that she'd left her suitcase (containing gifts for her children) at the airport's busy curb. She immediately asked Archangel Michael to surround her suitcase with his protective golden light. When she returned to the terminal, the piece of luggage was still where Carmen had left it.

Carmen says, "There were people coming and going, but no one seemed to notice the suitcase! It

was like it was enveloped in some invisible cloak, and no one had even touched it! I was so relieved and so grateful to Archangel Michael for his protective assistance."

Spiritual Protection

"Dear Archangel Michael, please surround me,
my loved ones, and my home with your royal purple
light to dissipate and ward off any lower energies.
Please guide me clearly so that I may only interact
with people who are living in truth and integrity."

Archangel Michael is *the* supreme protector who guards against all effects of fear and fear-based energies. After all, this negative emotion is the driving force behind everything that's unsavory in this world. Without fear, we have peace.

Michael will shield you from lower energies if you ask for his protection. Like a nightclub bouncer, he can keep fear-based spirits, experiences, and people away from you. There are just a couple of caveats: (1) you have to ask for his help, as I've been emphasizing; and (2) you need to listen to the intuitive feelings that warn you like red flags when you're around a lower-energy person or situation.

If your gut tells you that something is wrong in a relationship or situation, trust this feeling. It's your body's, your higher self's, Archangel Michael's, and God's way of warning you. And when that happens, you can ask Michael to lead you out of the situation. I can't emphasize this point strongly enough.

When parents ask me how to help their sensitive children sleep better, I counsel them to work with Archangel Michael. It's also a good idea to teach children to call upon him whenever they need extra courage or comfort.

When Jill Gunther's five-year-old daughter couldn't sleep, Archangel Michael came to their assistance. Jill knew there were lower energies in her daughter's bedroom because it was always cold, and she had nightmares whenever she slept in that room with her child. To her credit, Jill trusted these feelings.

Even after the family moved to a new home, her daughter's bedroom continued to be plagued by these energies. She realized that her highly sensitive daughter was attracting needy spirits.

So Jill sought out an Angel Therapist®, who called upon Archangel Michael to cut the cords of fear and clear the energy for her, her daughter, and every room in their home. Jill sensed Michael's energy and immediately felt at peace, as this was her first spiritual experience.

Since then, Jill's daughter has been sleeping well and has lost her fear of going to bed. The temperature of her bedroom now matches that of the rest of the house. And Jill's daughter knows that she can call upon Archangel Michael whenever she needs his strength and protection.

And adults need protection, too. If someone is angry with you or jealous of you, that person may be sending you "psychic attack" energy. Usually the attacking person has no idea of the force that his or her dark emotions carry. It's as if people are throwing fireballs when they harbor intense anger or jealousy toward another.

If you have sudden sharp pains, it could be a sign that you've been psychically attacked by someone. Even our loved ones inadvertently attack us at times. In fact, you may even attack *yourself* with unloving thoughts.

Archangel Michael can intercept incoming psychic attacks, shield you from further ones, and clear away the energy and impact of assaults that may have already reached you.

A woman named Gladys had been plagued by dark energies and psychic attacks since she was a child. Her mind spontaneously filled with disturbing and intrusive thoughts. Gladys tried everything for protection, shielding, and clearing, but it wasn't until she read about Archangel Michael and asked him to stay with her continuously that the torment stopped.

Gladys told me, "The attacks are gone. Archangel Michael is a wonderful friend. Since he's been with me, I feel an elevation in my own vibration."

Protecting Job and Reputation

"Archangel Michael, thank you for protecting my career and reputation from lower energies. Please guide my actions so that they reflect the highest integrity and my true spiritual path."

Archangel Michael protects us in many ways, including guarding our reputation and job status, as Carol Clausen discovered.

One day when Carol was a teacher's aide working toward her teaching credential, she had an ethical dilemma: The teacher she was working with in a classroom had to leave to attend to her own child. That left Carol in charge of the class, which was illegal in her state since she wasn't certified to teach. She worried that if she agreed to illegally watch the classroom, her reputation would be marred and she'd be barred from teaching in the future.

So Carol asked Archangel Michael to protect her job and reputation by bringing in a certified teacher. As soon as she said this prayer, she heard a voice in her mind say, *Go look at the name on the folder that is on the chair where you left your coat!* So Carol lifted her coat and gasped in delight as she found the top folder had the name "Mike'l Archangel" on it!

With this sign, Carol was reassured that her prayer had been heard and answered. Sure enough, a moment later the school principal escorted a certified teacher into the classroom to teach for the day.

Life-Purpose Guidance

"Archangel Michael, what changes would you like to see me make in my life right now? Please clearly guide me upon the path of my life purpose."

Archangel Michael has been overseeing God's mission on Earth since before people populated the planet, and he lovingly oversees our human Divine life missions. Michael is a record keeper and manager, helping you (and everyone else) know the purpose of your life. He also guides your next step and helps you make important life changes.

Michael will guide your spiritually based career if you ask him, as Melanie Orders did. Melanie detested her job as an airport chef, especially the fact that she began work at 3 A.M. every day. A qualified remedial massage therapist, she dreamed of making massage her full-time career. But she hadn't done anything proactive to turn that dream into a reality.

Then Melanie learned that Archangel Michael could guide her healing career. So she asked him to help her move out of her chef job and begin getting massage clients. This prayer worked immediately! That day a workmate of Melanie's husband asked if he knew of a good massage therapist. *Voilà!* Melanie had her first massage client.

In the same way, Melanie began getting more massage referrals. Her practice grew, and she was able to reduce her hours at the airport. Melanie thanked Archangel Michael and asked him to help her do massage on a full-time basis.

Soon after making this request, Melanie had more synchronistic opportunities to massage people. Her husband also found a wonderful massage clinic available for rent, so Melanie was able to open a full-time practice and leave her airport job.

Melanie continues to work with Archangel Michael to clear the energy of her clinic, and to gain confidence in her ability to give angelic messages to her clients. Everything that she asked for has come true, thanks to Archangel Michael.

You can have similar success by partnering with Michael. It only requires asking him for help and guidance. Keep in mind that Melanie was immediately successful because she was crystal clear about what she wanted. If your prayers seem blocked or slow, it could be because you aren't sure what to ask for. Or perhaps you keep changing your mind. The clearer you are with Michael, the faster your dreams will manifest.

If you need clarity about your life purpose or career, I recommend taking a pen and pad of paper to a quiet place. Write a question to Archangel Michael. Then record the answer, which will come as a thought, a feeling, words, or visions. Jot down these impressions even if you don't understand them or you think you're making them up (you're not). In this written "interview" with Archangel Michael, you'll receive detailed guidance about your career or any topic you ask him about.

You can also ask Michael to give you guidance while you're sleeping. Simply think about the topic you'd like help with and ask him to come to you in your dreams. Request that his dream guidance be clear, understandable, and something you'll remember upon waking up.

Repairing Necessary Items

> *"Archangel Michael, thank you for*
> *fixing this item so that I can utilize it in*
> *the service of my Divine life purpose."*

These days, we're accustomed to relying upon computers and other mechanical and electrical tools. So if something malfunctions, it can interfere with our work and cause unnecessary stress. Archangel Michael has a particular talent for reviving these items, particularly if doing so supports our life purpose or provides protection.

For example, Terrick Heckstall's car headlights hadn't been working for five months, which was fine since he only drove to work during daylight hours. One day, though, an obligation kept Terrick in the office until sundown.

Terrick worried about driving in the dark without headlights—until he remembered to thank God and Archangel Michael for protection. As soon as he did, Terrick heard a loud, calming male voice (whom he believes was Michael) say, "Worry not. We'll provide the light." A moment later, Terrick's headlights miraculously came on, and he drove safely home, illuminated by Divine light!

Many people have told me how Michael miraculously intervened and helped their automobiles run safely. I've also heard stories of how the angels caused a car to stall out to avoid an accident. Michael knows what he's doing in order to protect us.

Elizabeth Pfeiffer, her husband, and son were off-roading with their new truck in four-wheel drive. But when they returned to the street, Elizabeth's husband couldn't switch the truck back to two-wheel drive. He tried pushing all of the buttons, and they studied the owners' manual, but nothing worked. They feared ruining the transmission by keeping the vehicle in four-wheel drive too long.

They were in a secluded location with no service stations, so Elizabeth decided to call upon Archangel Michael, who is renowned for fixing such problems. Elizabeth silently asked, *Archangel Michael, can you help us get the truck out of four-wheel drive?*

The truck slipped right back into two-wheel drive! Elizabeth's husband stared at the console in surprise and said, "It's back! It's in two-wheel drive now!"

Elizabeth asked, "Did you hit the button?"

With a surprised look on his face, he answered, "No, it just came back on!"

They drove for several moments and were talking about how miraculously the button had clicked into gear when their son spoke up from the backseat and said, "You know, I called Archangel Michael to help us."

With a gasp, Elizabeth said, "Me, too!" and they high-fived each other to celebrate their angelic teamwork.

Archangel Michael can repair any electronic or mechanical item. He either gives intuitive guidance as to how to fix it yourself, leads you to the right repair person, or intervenes and fixes it himself. I always trust that Michael knows what he's doing and will choose the best method for supporting and helping us.

For instance, when Nicholas Davis's office was upgrading the memory disks in their computers, he and his colleague struggled to open a computer case, which was screwed on tightly with old fasteners. They tried every possible way to open the case, but it was fused shut.

Finally, Nicholas remembered his previous successes in asking Archangel Michael to fix electronic equipment. Nicholas called upon him silently and then felt Michael's energy so strongly that it overwhelmed his whole body. He heard the words: *I am here to assist you with your computer.*

Nicholas was then able to open the computer

case within two seconds! He doesn't even recall how he did it. It just happened.

Nicholas's colleague, puzzled, looked at him and asked, "Wow, how on earth did you do that?"

Nicholas decided to tell the truth and replied fearlessly, "I didn't do anything. I called upon the angels, and they opened it for me."

Over the years, I've received stories of Michael fixing plumbing, electronic locks, iPods, and countless other devices. The common denominator among all these stories? The person asked Michael for help!

Signs from Archangel Michael

"Dear Archangel Michael, please send me a clear sign that I will easily notice and understand, letting me know you are here and helping me gain guidance and peace about this situation."

Each archangel emanates a halo or energy field. You know that energy can vibrate at different rates, creating the appearance of different colors. Well, each archangel's different energies make for different-colored halos.

Archangel Michael's halo is a rich royal purple or royal blue, and also golden, light. Some visually sensitive people actually see flashes or sparkles of these colors with their physical eyes. This is one sign that Michael is around you. Another is if you're suddenly attracted to items with the royal blue-purple coloring.

A woman named Nadine called on Archangel Michael for protection one night as she sat in her car alone in a dark parking lot while her husband ran an errand. As soon as Nadine asked Michael for help, she saw a tall blue flourescent shadow standing next to her. The vision only lasted a few seconds, but it was enough to reassure Nadine that she was safe, which she was.

Because Michael has a fiery sword of light that he uses in service of the Divine, he emits a lot of heat. So if you feel intense heat, it's another sign that Michael is with you.

Michael isn't shy. When he's present, he'll let you clearly know, as Amber Armstrong discovered.

When friends suggested that Amber watch the movie *Michael,* she agreed. After all, she'd just had a vision of the archangel that was very John Travolta–like. Yet, she had never seen the film.

So when Amber called her local Target store to inquire if they had the movie in stock, she was only a little surprised when her call was answered by a man saying, "This is Michael—how may I help you?"

Michael, the Target employee, found that there was one copy of the *Michael* movie in the back storeroom and not on the shelves. Amber drove there immediately and bought the movie, and now she feels closer to Archangel Michael than ever.

Stories such as Amber's really show what a wonderful sense of humor Michael has.

Some Have Entertained Angels Unawares . . .

The famous quotation from the biblical Paul advising us to be careful when entertaining strangers, for "some have entertained angels unawares," speaks to the fact that sometimes angels take on human appearances in order to help us.

Hundreds of people have told me of meeting a mysterious stranger with unusual eyes who utters just the right comforting words, or who rescues them in some way. He's been described as tall, sometimes well dressed and sometimes shabbily dressed. He's also been described as being of different races. Very often he introduces himself as "Michael." This stranger then disappears without a trace, and no one can ever find him again.

Take Candace Pruitt-Heckstall's experience, for example. It had been months since Candace had ridden the bus. As she stood at the bus stop in freezing weather, she worried whether her bus would come or if she'd missed it. Candace also fretted about getting off at the right stop to reach her destination.

To ease her mind, Candace silently thanked God and Archangel Michael for sending the bus along quickly. A moment later, a tall, pleasant man with very unusual eyes stopped to talk to Candace. She marveled that his eyes were so filled with sunlight even though his back was to the dim winter sun. His words and presence comforted Candace, and soon her worries were gone.

Before Candace stepped onto the bus, she introduced herself to the man, who then told her that his name was Mike. When she turned to wave goodbye to him, he had vanished. Candace is certain that Archangel Michael sent his namesake to calm her. Since then, she has felt no more anxiety about riding the bus.

Clearing and Shielding

Archangel Michael is a master at working with earthly energies for our protection and benefit. This is essential for highly sensitive people who can pick up on the energy of anger or competitiveness, for example, from other people or in buildings. Those who are highly sensitive often absorb other people's energies like a sponge taking on dirty dishwater.

If you're highly sensitive, then you probably have mood and energy swings. One minute you're up and excited about life, and the next you can't get out of bed. The only way to stabilize your mood and energy is by managing your energy field. And Michael can help you with this.

Anytime you feel down or tired, this is a sign that you've absorbed other people's fear-based energies. This is the time to say silently or aloud: "Archangel Michael, please clear me inside and out." You may feel tingles, shivers, or twitches as lower energies are released following this request.

Once your body feels calm, then it's time to say, "Archangel Michael, please shield me," as a protective measure. He'll surround you in a cocoon of his royal blue-purple halo light. Always ask Michael to shield you before entering into any harsh situation.

Archangel Michael is strongly palpable and present in daily life. As you work with him, you'll

find him to be profoundly reliable and a trust-
worthy mentor, partner, and sacred being. In the
next chapter, we'll connect with the healer of the
angelic realm: Archangel Raphael.

Chapter Two

RAPHAEL

*"Dear Archangel Raphael, thank you
for infusing me and my loved ones with
your healing light of God's pure love."*

Raphael is also known as: Azarias, Israfel, or Labbiel

Raphael's name means: "God heals"

Raphael has long been regarded as the angel of healing. His name may be derived from the Hebrew word *Rophe*, which means "medicine doctor"; or *Rapach*, which means "God heals the soul."

As I explained in my book *The Healing Miracles of Archangel Raphael*, although Raphael isn't named in the Bible, theologians believe he was the archangel who healed the infirm at the Bethesda pond described in the Gospels. He is also thought to be one of the three angels who visited the patriarch Abraham and his wife, Sarah, to help with their conception; as well as the angel who healed Abraham's grandson Jacob's wrestling injuries and who gave King Solomon his magical ring.

In Catholicism, he is Saint Raphael, the patron of physicians, travelers, and matchmakers. Raphael appears by name in the Book of Tobit. This scriptural work, sometimes called the Book of Tobias, was lost and later rediscovered as a Dead Sea Scroll in Qumran, the temple of the ancient Essenes, in 1952.

The book describes the story of Tobit, a devoted and helpful Jewish man who was in such despair when he went blind that he asked God to let him die. The same evening of Tobit's prayer, a woman named Sarah also begged God for death, out of grief for her seven husbands, who had each died on her wedding night.

So God answered both Tobit's and Sarah's prayers by sending Archangel Raphael in human form. Raphael didn't identify himself as an angel, but instead offered to protect and guide Tobit's son Tobias as he journeyed to retrieve money that was owed to him.

Raphael led Tobias to Sarah, and the two fell in love and married. Using fish as part of his healing work, Raphael then helped Tobias successfully cast off the demons that had killed Sarah's previous husbands. He also used an ointment made from fish to help Tobias heal his father's blindness. As Tobit, Tobias, and Sarah enjoyed their new life, Raphael retrieved Tobit's money. Once his work was done, the archangel revealed his true identity and returned to the angelic realm.

His name also appears in another Dead Sea Scroll text, the Book of Enoch, in which his role upon Earth is described as "one of the holy angels, who is over the spirits of men." In this book, the Lord charges Raphael with the task of healing Earth of the mess made by some fallen angels and giants, binding and casting out a demon, helping all of the children, and saving the world from corruption. Archangel Raphael is still focused on this mission today.

In Islamic scriptures, Raphael is known as Israfel, the archangel who is destined to blow a large horn twice to signal Judgment Day. Legend holds that Raphael's original name was Labbiel. When Labbiel sided with God on the question of whether to create humans, the Lord rewarded the angel by changing his name to Raphael.

Raphael, the Angelic Physician

Archangel Raphael brings God's healing light to Earth. He once told me in a meditation that rather than *healing,* his role consisted of *revealing* the true healed bodies that God created for all of us. To Raphael, everyone is already healthy in spiritual truth.

Immediate Healings

"Thank you, Archangel Raphael, for healing me completely right now."

When you ask Raphael to heal a condition, often the cure manifests instantly. The archangel was just waiting for you to give him permission to conduct his healing work.

For example, Keiko Tanaka and her husband live in a very small Canadian town, so they plan their outings to the big city to accomplish banking, shopping, and other errands all in the same day. At the beginning of one such busy outing, Keiko began to feel very ill, and she immediately appealed to Archangel Raphael for help. With her eyes open, Keiko saw an oval-shaped emerald green light about the size of a child. After that, her sickness was gone! She and her husband enjoyed the rest of their busy day, and Keiko thanked Raphael profusely.

The emerald light that Keiko saw is the halo color of Archangel Raphael. His energy sparkles or flashes bright green—which, interestingly, is the same color that Eastern mystics see in the heart-chakra energy center. So the emerald green signifies that Raphael is infusing you with pure Divine love energy.

Sometimes people feel a gentle buzzing energy as Raphael is healing them; or they see green lights, as Keiko did. But for others, like Elizabeth Macarthur, Raphael's healing is very subtle.

When Elizabeth asked her doctor why she was tired all the time, she was diagnosed with sleep apnea and told to go to bed with a mask hooked to oxygen. It took some time for her to adjust to sleeping with the mask, but she never did adjust to carrying the machine with her while traveling. After four years of using it, Elizabeth was tired of its noise and the way it would fall off while she was asleep.

About this time, Elizabeth discovered that Archangel Raphael could help heal her condition, so she asked for his assistance. Shortly thereafter, the machine began malfunctioning, and Elizabeth's energy level was good even though she wasn't sleeping with the mask. She realized that Raphael had healed her, and she no longer needed the machine.

I believe that Elizabeth was healed while she was sleeping, which is true for many who receive such help from Raphael. The reason is that when you're asleep, you're much more open to the intense love that Raphael sends.

Angel Therapist Amy McRae had success in calling upon Archangel Raphael to heal her while sleeping. She discovered this method one day when she was feeling unbalanced and depleted and none of her family or friends was available to help her. So Amy took a nap and decided to ask Raphael to give her a full healing session while she slept. Amy slept very deeply and woke up feeling energized and healthy.

Referral to a Health-Care Provider

*"Dear Archangel Raphael, please guide me to
the best healer for my condition and situation,
and help me get an appointment right away."*

As common as it is to receive an instant healing from Raphael, sometimes he guides people to get their treatment from physicians and other health-care providers. In *The Healing Miracles of Archangel Raphael,* there's a story of a man who—after he asked

Archangel Raphael to help him with his health condition—was led to a physician named Dr. Raphael!

I've received stories of Raphael creating synchronicities that help people find the best healer for their condition. And, as the following story from Therese Zibara Slan illustrates, Raphael also ensures that you'll see this healer in a timely manner.

Therese always believed in angels, but it took a major health crisis for her to truly know how much they love and support us.

During the summer of 1999, she was too busy completing reports at work to take care of her health, even though she'd recently developed serious symptoms. Finally, her boss and co-worker urged her to see a doctor, who took tests. When the results came in, the doctor called Therese to say that she needed to get to the hospital immediately, as her condition was life threatening.

Nine patients were ahead of Therese at the emergency room, so she sat patiently, even though she was losing consciousness. But she needn't have worried, as she saw a clear vision of Archangel Raphael personally healing all of the people who were in the waiting room. One by one, the nine patients ahead of her left the ER before the doctor could see them—due to Raphael's expert healing care!

When Therese was admitted, she passed out and immediately saw a bright white light and her departed grandfather, who communicated that it wasn't yet her time to cross over. The doctors and nurses in attendance were able to revive her, thanks to Raphael speeding up the hospital-admittance process.

Pain Management

"Thank you, Archangel Raphael, for helping me feel good, and comfortable in my body."

Raphael can help you reduce or eliminate pain stemming from short-term and chronic conditions. Again, it's a result of your asking for his help. In this way, you signal your permission for him to intervene.

I've received many stories from people who asked Raphael to accompany them to the dentist's office, always with glowing results. For instance, Kim Hutchinson nearly canceled her dental appointment because the past few had been so emotionally and physically painful. Not only did the cleanings hurt her sensitive gums, but the hygienists invariably hurt her feelings by repeatedly questioning whether she really flossed regularly (she did!) based upon her gums' poor health.

As the dental appointment grew near, Kim felt anxious and ill. But instead of canceling, she called upon Archangel Raphael for help. Kim asked Raphael for a pain-free cleaning; a sympathetic hygienist; and most important, healthy gums and teeth. Kim felt these wishes were pie-in-the-sky dreams but decided, *What have I got to lose?*

The date of the appointment arrived, and Kim set off with trepidation. She kept praying silently to Raphael to help with the appointment, and she could feel his presence and see his green energy nearby. Then a hygienist whom Kim had never met entered the lobby, and Kim thought, *She looks so kind. Please, Raphael, let her be my hygienist.* Sure enough, she called Kim's name. The hygienist was soft-spoken and had a gentle, soothing manner that Kim found reassuring.

It was only when the woman started to clean Kim's teeth that her anxiety returned. She braced for the pain, but there was none! Eventually she allowed herself to relax. After the hygienist polished and flossed her teeth, she asked her about her flossing habits. Certain that the hygienist was going to question her credibility, Kim tensed again. But instead, she complimented her on her flossing and brushing routine, and said that Kim's gums were looking much healthier than her chart indicated.

Kim was elated! For the first time in four years, she received a "passing grade" at the dentist's office. Kim felt the presence of angels, and heard them whisper that the hygienist was an Earth angel. Kim knew in that instant that her dental woes were over! Archangel Raphael had fixed her gums and alleviated her phobia of dental care.

Travel Help

"Thank you, Archangel Raphael, for accompanying me and my travel companions on our trip, helping us and our belongings arrive safely at our destination."

Since the time of his journey with Tobias, Raphael has been regarded as the patron of travelers. As someone who travels frequently, I can attest to Raphael's talents in ensuring a smooth trip.

The testimonials I've received, and my own experiences, show that you can ask Raphael for help with smoothing airplane turbulence, receiving cooperation from airline and hotel clerks, and getting your luggage quickly when your flight lands.

Raphael also combines his healing and travel talents to assure that you stay well prior to and during your vacation. For example, Billie Quantrell and her husband, Chad, were getting ready to take a vacation when he came down with a nasty flu. So Billie called upon Archangel Raphael for help. She prayed, *Whatever lesson is to be learned, please hurry it along, as this illness is taking a toll on Chad.* She then visualized Raphael's emerald green energy entering her husband's body through his crown chakra, at the top of his head. Chad recovered quickly, and they were able to enjoy their vacation.

Raphael is a traveling physician who makes house calls wherever you are in the world.

Giving Hope and Comfort

For whatever reason, some health conditions persist. Whether you want to call it karma, the soul's choice, or destiny, it seems that some people don't receive complete healings when they ask for them. In these situations, Raphael works to ensure the person's comfort. He minimizes pain and buoys the spirits.

For instance, during the 20 years that Sarah McKechnie has suffered with a life-threatening autoimmune disease, she's cried out for Archangel

Raphael's help as she struggled with searing pain and the fear of death.

Raphael's presence has filled Sarah with hope in times of despair. She says, "This disease has taught me that angelic help is alive and well, because in those times of greatest suffering—where the only thing I could do was throw myself into the arms of the angels—they were always there to catch me." Sarah is grateful for the help Raphael gives her. Although her condition persists, she has managed to find peace, which is the greatest gift of all.

Healing Pets

In addition to healing and comforting people, Archangel Raphael also ministers to animals. He heals injuries and illnesses in all types of creatures. I've found that pets respond very quickly to Raphael's healing work. They drink in the archangel's energy like a healing elixir, and they regain their health rapidly as a result.

Debbie was devastated when her beloved Akita/shepherd mix, Kiko, tore a ligament in his leg. As she waited for her veterinarian's office to open, she sat with the dog, begging God and Archangel Raphael for help.

Instinctively, Debbie held her hand a few inches above Kiko's injured leg. Debbie says that as she pleaded with Raphael for aid, "with my physical eyes open, I saw what can best be described as a green miniature bolt of lightning emanate from my palm to Kiko's thigh." She fervently thanked Raphael for this validation of his presence and continued to send the dog healing energy. (You'll recall that Raphael's halo color is green, and that when people see this green light, it's a sign of his healing presence.)

Then Debbie and Kiko fell asleep. When they awoke an hour later, Debbie trembled with excitement as she discovered a beautiful pure-white eight-inch-long feather lying on Kiko's thigh!

There was no other explanation than that Raphael had left a physical sign that Kiko would be all right. And he was: not only did his leg heal, but he lived to the ripe old age of 15, which is highly unusual for a big dog. Debbie gives all credit to God and Archangel Raphael.

Raphael also ensures our pets' safety by watching over them when we're away or when they're outside. You can ask Raphael to protect your beloved pets. You can also ask him to bring wayward animals home. Raphael is brilliant at locating lost dogs, cats, and other critters.

For example, Ann McWilliam's four cats like to wander outside during the day, so she calls on Archangel Raphael to keep them nearby and then to get them back inside. The cats love the freedom of nature, and they love coming back into the house. If Ann's cats are out of sight, she calls upon Raphael to help, and her cats appear and eagerly run back inside.

Guiding Healers

"Thank you, Archangel Raphael, for guiding my healing career and helping me bring blessings to everyone I encounter."

As the patron saint of physicians, Raphael helps both traditional and alternative healers. If you feel called to one of these professions, you can ask Raphael to help you decide which branch of healing work you'd most enjoy and excel in. Notice any books that mysteriously fall off shelves around you, as that's usually a sign from Raphael.

At your request, the archangel can also help you select a school and obtain the time and money for your healing education. Upon graduation, he'll assist

you with securing a healing practice or other outlet for your work in your chosen area. Raphael can help you attract wonderful clients as well.

When you're conducting healing work, call upon Raphael to guide your words and actions. You'll receive intuitive ideas, visions, and feelings—which are God's healing wisdom, delivered through the archangel.

Calling Upon Raphael on Behalf of Someone Else

"Dear Archangel Raphael, please attend to [name of person] *and help him/her be healthy, happy, and strong. Please guide me as to how I can help as well."*

You can ask Archangel Raphael for healing help for another person. He won't violate the other person's free will. So, if the individual doesn't want to be healed for some reason, Raphael can't usurp this decision. However, he'll stay by the person because you asked, which will have beneficial effects.

Archangel Raphael often works in tandem with Archangel Michael to clear away fear and stress, which are major factors affecting health. The more you work with these archangels, the more you'll come to trust them. In our next chapter, we'll work with another well-known archangel: Gabriel.

Chapter Three

GABRIEL

*"Dear Archangel Gabriel, thank you for giving
me clear messages about* [issue at hand] *and
for guiding and supporting me to be a clear
messenger to help others, as you do."*

Gabriel is also known as: Saint Gabriel, Jibril,
or Jiburili

Gabriel's name means: "The strength of God"

Gabriel is one of two archangels specifically
named in the Bible (the other being Michael). In the
Old Testament's Book of Daniel, Gabriel appears to
Daniel to help him understand his visions of the
future. In the New Testament's Gospels, Gabriel

appears in the Book of Luke in famous scenes called the Annunciation, because the archangel announces the forthcoming births of John the Baptist and Jesus Christ.

When the archangel tells Zechariah of his future son, John the Baptist, the man is amazed because he thought he and his wife, Elizabeth, were too old to bear children. The archangel reassures him by saying, "I am Gabriel. I stand in the presence of God, and I have been sent to speak to you and to tell you this good news." Soon after, Gabriel goes to Mary and says, "Behold, I bring you good tidings of great joy," and proceeds to describe her future son, Jesus Christ.

Gabriel also appears in the apocryphal Book of Enoch, as a messenger between humanity and God.

In Islamic faith, the archangel Gabriel revealed the Qur'an scripture to the prophet Muhammad.

These scriptural roles underscore Gabriel's mission as the supreme messenger of God, and why this archangel is the patron saint of communications workers.

Artists throughout time have portrayed the angel in the Annunciation and other images of Gabriel with feminine features, long hair, flowing gowns, and—if you look closely at the Renaissance

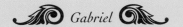
paintings—a feminine figure. Perhaps this is because Gabriel is so closely aligned with the Divine feminine situations of pregnancy, birth, and communication.

Of course, angels have no true gender identification since they don't have physical bodies. However, their energy is distinctly male or female according to their specialties, with Archangel Michael being a perfect example of traditional brawny male strength. Gabriel, in contrast, exudes soft, nurturing, feminine strength.

Nurturing Our Children

"Archangel Gabriel, thank you for helping me parent my beloved child. Please watch over me and my little one, ensuring our health and happiness."

Gabriel and Mother Mary work closely together to minister to sensitive children. They guide conceptions, adoptions, pregnancies, births, and the raising of children.

For example, Diane Fordham has found Archangel Gabriel to be wonderfully supportive in parenting her two-year-old daughter. When her toddler

acts out and Diane struggles for patience, she calls upon Gabriel. Instantly, she feels surrounded by much-needed calmness, which positively affects her child in turn. Soon, both mother and daughter are peaceful and smiling.

Recently, Diane's daughter was tired and cranky, but she still wouldn't sleep. So Diane said to Gabriel, "My daughter needs to sleep, and so do I. Please help us." She then took a few deep breaths, and without thinking, she found herself humming a lullaby that she hadn't sung since her daughter was a tiny baby. The lullaby calmed the little girl instantly, and they both closed their eyes and slept.

Life Purpose Involving Children

"Dear Archangel Gabriel, please guide me to a meaningful career that will fully support me while I bring blessings to the children of the world."

Because Gabriel is deeply concerned about children's welfare, the archangel mentors responsible and loving adults who wish to help the young. If you feel called to work with children in any capacity, please ask Gabriel to help you.

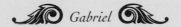

Clear Messages

"Thank you, Archangel Gabriel, for giving me crystal clear guidance about [describe the topic]."

Gabriel is usually portrayed with a large copper trumpet, to symbolize clearly trumpeting messages from God. If you need a message with specific details, call upon Archangel Gabriel.

As an Angel Therapist, Hilda Blair (whose story of being protected by Archangel Michael while driving was relayed in Chapter 1) knows which archangels to call upon for specific purposes. So when she wants clear messages, she calls upon none other than *the* messenger angel, Gabriel.

One day Hilda did just that when she felt ready to start dating again after a breakup. Through her thoughts and intuition, she received Gabriel's guidance to go to the mall as a way of meeting someone. Jokingly, Hilda said to Gabriel aloud, "What? Am I going to be walking along and some guy is going to tap me on the shoulder and ask me where Sears is?" Hilda laughed at this silly notion, but decided to go to the mall anyway.

And as Hilda was walking in the middle of the shopping center, a tall, nice-looking man tapped her

on the shoulder and said, "Could you tell me where Sears is?" Hilda was so shocked that her conversation with Gabriel had come true exactly that all she could do was grin and point in the direction of Sears.

Hilda realized that Gabriel had answered her question about where to meet a guy very clearly. Unfortunately, by the time she recovered from her surprise, it was too late to locate the tall man. However, this experience helped her realize that the archangel *was* clearly giving her messages and would continue to do so in every area of her life. Hilda's story also shows Gabriel's sense of humor and amazing creativity.

Helping Other Messengers

"Archangel Gabriel, please mentor, guide, and support my career as a messenger of [give specific details] and help me shine Divine light and love upon others through this career."

Gabriel helps earthly messengers such as teachers, counselors, writers, artists, and actors. The archangel acts like a Heavenly agent and manager who motivates you to polish your skills. Gabriel then opens the door of opportunity for you to work in

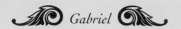

your chosen career, and gives you a loving push through it if you hesitate.

Before people ask Gabriel for career help, I always explain that this archangel will nudge and motivate you to work hard on your messenger calling, always with wonderful rewards. I remember one woman who asked the archangel to help her finish her book. Well, Gabriel made sure that the woman stayed awake for several days and nights until it was finished!

In a similar way, Gabriel inspired Barbara Hewitt to write. As Barbara was getting out of the shower one morning, she heard a voice give her seven book titles. She knew right away that these were children's books that she was destined to pen. Barbara sat each day with a large pad of paper and asked Archangel Gabriel to help her write them. Upon that request, the thoughts flowed . . . and Barbara wrote all seven books. She credits Gabriel with giving her the guidance to know how to complete them. She says that each book emanates the love of God.

Whether your messenger work is by the written or spoken word, Archangel Gabriel can guide you. For example, Kristy M. Ayala, an Angel Therapist who holds a master's degree, was a faculty member at a university in California. She enjoyed lecturing

about psychology to her students. However, she longed to incorporate more spirituality into her career. Kristy trained to become a spiritual counselor and quit her job to perform one-on-one counseling sessions. While she enjoyed this work, she missed teaching.

So Kristy asked Archangel Gabriel, the angel who helps teachers and messengers, for guidance. While meditating and praying, she received a clear message that she could do both spiritual *and* teaching work. So Kristy asked Gabriel to help her find venues and students, which would allow her to teach and lecture again—but this time about spiritual topics. Kristy heard the message that she should trust. If she did so, all of the right doors would open for her.

Kristy surrendered the entire situation to God and Archangel Gabriel, although she didn't have a clue about how to move forward with being a spiritual teacher. And just as she'd heard in meditation, the doors started opening for Kristy!

She recalls, "People began asking me if I'd give a lecture about the archangels. I was so happy, and very surprised because I'd known these people for some time and they'd never before asked me to teach anything like that." So Kristy said yes, and her archangel workshop was a success! Out of this, she

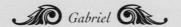
received more invitations to speak about angels at schools and healing centers.

Kristy talks to Gabriel all the time, and the angel has taught her that she can experience all the components of work that she loves, and that she doesn't need to trade one aspect for another. Thanks to Gabriel, Kristy has a very fulfilling career doing what she loves.

Gabriel also knows that the media is a conduit for delivering loving messages. So the archangel will gladly help you communicate them through television, newspapers, magazines, books, radio, or the Internet.

For example, Karen Forrest was scheduled to appear on live TV promoting her book, and she was naturally nervous about being articulate. So she silently called upon Gabriel, asking, *Archangel Gabriel, please release me from this worry and nervousness about my live interview. Speak through me during the interview so I don't have to think about it or worry about what to say. Be with me, Archangel Gabriel, every step of the way and act as my public-relations agent. Thanks, Archangel Gabriel.*

After thinking these words, Karen felt a sense of peace sweep through her and the physical sensation of an angel wing touching her shoulder. The worry

and nervousness were released! Karen knew within her heart that Archangel Gabriel would be by her side during the TV appearance.

Following the interview, the host commented on the fact that she had interviewed many people and was impressed by how relaxed Karen had been on live television and how easily their conversation had flowed.

Signs from Gabriel

As described earlier, each archangel has a specific purpose. This means that each has a different energy vibration. Just as different colors vibrate at different rates, the archangels' halo colors vary.

Gabriel's halo is copper colored, like the angel's symbolic trumpet. If you see flashes or sparkles of copper light, or if you find yourself suddenly attracted to this metal, this is a sign that you're working with Archangel Gabriel.

An obstetric nurse named Carmen Carignan—who helps with underwater-birth deliveries in New Hampshire (and who was also mentioned in Chapter 1 because Archangel Michael protected her suitcase at the airport)—saw the copper "signs" when she asked for Gabriel's help.

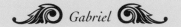

When Carmen wanted to open a healing practice, she called upon Archangel Gabriel for guidance. She knew that Gabriel, as the archangel of communication, often announces what's on the horizon, and acts like a manager or agent in orchestrating new ventures related to one's soul purpose.

Immediately, Carmen received signs of Gabriel's involvement. First, she found orange-copper colored feathers twice without a logical explanation. The second sign was a photo developed of Carmen with a definite copper and white angel-shaped orb next to her. The angel in the photo was so clear that the photo-lab people were talking about it!

And the third *very exciting* sign was when a local massage therapist telephoned Carmen to tell her about an affordable room in a healing center that was now vacant and ready to lease. Carmen knew that Archangel Gabriel had arranged for the massage therapist to learn about the space and about Carmen's desire, and then to find her telephone number. It was all beyond coincidence, and this miracle exceeded Carmen's expectations.

Carmen says, "When I surrendered to the assistance of this communication angel, everything was put into place effortlessly and rather quickly. I'm still amazed!"

Of course, Gabriel will work with you the moment you ask, even if you don't notice these signs. A woman named Maryne Hachey desperately wanted to see Gabriel and the other angels. Maryne had been trying to connect with them and had been working on the exercises in the book *Angel Visions*. But she realized she was trying too hard to see angels. Fortunately, her mind was relaxed enough while she was sleeping one night to allow her to clearly interact with Archangel Gabriel.

In the dream, Maryne stood beneath a beautiful cherry tree in full bloom, on a street that had no beginning or end. The dream was so real that she could smell the cherry blossoms and feel the breeze on her skin. The breeze blew flowers and feathers down the street, and Maryne's heart was filled with a profound sense of love.

Then a large female angel appeared. Her hair was blonde and wild, and she was accompanied by three other angels. The large angel stretched out her hand and said to Maryne, "You are on the right path."

With tears of gratitude running down her face, Maryne asked, "Who are you?"

The female angel replied, "Gabriel," and the cherry blossoms turned into white feathers, which fell to the ground where Maryne stood.

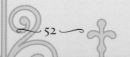

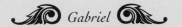
With that, Maryne woke with joy and excitement, knowing that the archangel had blessed her with love.

Gabriel is a hardworking, tenacious angel who promotes the same work ethic in those who ask for help. In our next chapter, we'll connect with Archangel Uriel, who will give us wonderful insights and ideas.

Chapter Four

URIEL

*"Archangel Uriel, thank you for giving me
information, ideas, and insight about* [topic
you want to know more about]*."*

Uriel is also known as: Aretziel, Auriel, Nuriel,
or Phanuel

Uriel's name means: "The Light of God"

When most people think of archangels, they include Uriel in the list. Yet, this archangel seems the most mysterious; and eludes the clear definitions accorded to Michael, Raphael, and Gabriel.

Uriel is named in Christian Gnostic scripture, as well as in the apocryphal book 2 Esdras, wherein

he teaches the prophet Ezra the meaning of esoteric information and the answers to metaphysical questions. This helped Ezra have meaningful conversations with God.

In the Book of Enoch, Uriel is one of the archangels who protected humankind from the Watchers (a group of fallen angels), including guiding the prophet Enoch, who later ascended into the archangel realm as Metatron.

Uriel's sainthood was revoked in 745 by Pope Zachary, who only allowed titles for angels named in the canonical scriptures (Michael, Raphael, and Gabriel). However, the Anglican church continues to venerate Uriel as the patron saint of the Sacrament of Confirmation.

Christian theology holds that Uriel rescued the infant John the Baptist from the "massacre of the innocents," and continued to be a guide to him and his mother, Elizabeth, as they left Egypt.

Archangel Uriel is depicted in paintings and Christian theology as a cherub; and in my visions of him, he's shorter and chubbier than the other archangels. As the "Light of God," he often holds a lantern that emits pale yellow candlelight.

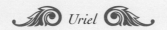

The Intellectual Archangel

*"Dear Archangel Uriel, please help me
focus my mind and receive all of the knowledge,
wisdom, and understanding that I need."*

Uriel illuminates our minds with information,
ideas, epiphanies, and insights. He reminds me of
a wise old uncle in this way. He's wonderful to call
upon whenever you need a solution, such as at business meetings, when writing, while studying, or
when taking a test. He'll whisper correct and appropriate answers into your ear, which you'll receive as
words or thoughts that are suddenly "downloaded"
into your mind. After you ask Uriel for help, notice
your thoughts. You can trust what you get as the
right answer, directly from the archangel.

Karen Forrest (whose Archangel Gabriel experience was described in the last chapter) calls upon
Archangel Uriel to help her remember names and
other information. Recently, a familiar-looking woman approached her at a workshop. Not recalling how
to address her, Karen silently asked Uriel, *What's this
woman's first name?* Immediately, Karen heard *Lynda*
in her head, and was able to greet the woman by her
correct first name.

Another time, a friend recommended a book, but Karen didn't have a pen to write down the title. So she asked Uriel to remind her, and then she promptly forgot all about the book. Two weeks later when Karen was in a bookstore, her intuition told her to look on a certain bottom shelf. Although she usually avoided looking at low shelves because she didn't like to hunch over, Karen followed her intuition. Sure enough, the book her friend had recommended was there! It answered many of Karen's spiritual questions.

So you can call upon Uriel to guide your intellectual pursuits. He works in tandem with the archangel Zadkiel to help students excel on tests and in school.

Radleigh Valentine discovered that Archangel Uriel was his main guide when he took my Angel Therapy Practitioner® course several years ago. I led the class through a meditation where I brought in each of the 15 archangels alphabetically.

As I named and meditated upon each archangel, Radleigh felt nothing—until I got to Uriel. As soon as I mentioned that archangel's name, Radleigh saw an explosion of golden light, as if the floor had turned into golden glitter and a light was illuminating the middle of the room. He could practically hear the angels singing! And then when I moved on to

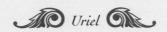
Archangel Zadkiel, all that music and light dropped away for Radleigh.

For the remainder of the class, Radleigh experienced readings and received oracle cards all pointing to Archangel Uriel's presence in his life. Now, he works with Uriel personally and professionally. For instance, the archangel helped Radleigh end a relationship peacefully and with love. And Uriel also helped him give a speech in front of hundreds of people, with glowing feedback from the audience. Uriel has also assisted him in making other positive changes in his life, such as leaving an unhealthy job situation. Now Radleigh calls Uriel the "Epiphany Angel" because he always offers such great ideas and guidance.

Just as Uriel guides Radleigh's public speeches, so too can he assist with the conversations you have with people. Angel Therapist Melanie Orders (whose story of receiving help from Archangel Michael in opening a massage practice appeared in Chapter 1) calls upon Archangel Uriel when she's working with someone who has a negative mind-set or low self-esteem. Melanie asks Uriel to guide the words she says to her clients, and he always helps her choose those that allow them to feel better about themselves. Melanie says that Uriel has guided her to develop better communication skills with all the people in her life, leading her to become an even kinder and more tactful person.

Archangel Uriel connects us to God's infinite wisdom and assists us in focusing upon intellectual pursuits. In the next chapter, we'll connect with Archangel Chamuel, who helps us locate whatever it is we're seeking.

Chapter Five

CHAMUEL

*"Thank you, Archangel Chamuel, for instilling me
with pure Divine peace, that I may rest in the knowledge
that you and God are watching over all of us."*

Chamuel is also known as: Camael, Camiel,
Camiul, Camniel, Chamael, Kamael, Khamael, or
KMAL

Chamuel's name means: "He who sees God"

Chamuel is one of the seven archangels of the
5th-century Pseudo-Dionysian teachings on the
celestial hierarchy. He is sometimes confused with
Samael, an "angel" who has dark and destruc-
tive leanings. The confusion likely stems from the

similar sound of their names. But rest assured that Chamuel is entirely of God's light.

In the Kabbalah, Chamuel (as Kamael) is the archangel of the *Geburah,* the fifth Sephirah (aspect of God) on the Tree of Life, denoting strength and courage through severity. Kabbalists consider Chamuel (Kamael) one of the Seraphim, which is the highest level of the choirs of angels.

As "he who sees God," Chamuel has omniscient vision, and he sees the connection between everyone and everything. His holy mission includes the manifestation of universal peace through helping individuals attain inner peace, even during turbulent times.

Chamuel uses his vision to ensure that you and others are at peace by helping you find what you're looking for. From his lofty vantage point, Chamuel can see the location of every missing item and the solutions to every problem. Even though he's stationed at an extremely high level, Chamuel is very down-to-earth and accessible, like a great man who has remained entirely humble.

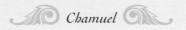

Chamuel, the Finding Angel

"Dear Archangel Chamuel, thank you for guiding me to find what I'm looking for, which includes [give specific details about your search].*"*

I receive the most letters from people who have had powerful angel experiences with Archangel Michael, who saves or protects them; with Archangel Raphael, who heals them; and with Archangel Chamuel, who helps them find something (in this descending order).

In this respect, Archangel Chamuel fulfills a role similar to Saint Anthony in Catholicism, who also helps reunite us with missing items. Both are amazingly swift at bringing back beloved heirloom items such as wedding rings.

If you're worried about bothering this angel with requests to find your car keys or eyeglasses, let me reassure you: Chamuel is happy to help! He's charged with a mighty mission of fulfilling universal peace, and part of this plan involves reducing human stress. So if you're stressed about losing something, rest assured that Chamuel wants to assist. To him, it's easy to locate your missing item, since he can see the location of *everything*.

Chamuel can help you find your life's purpose; a better job or home; your right relationship; and anything, esoteric or tangible, that you request, as long as it's in alignment with your higher self's path. He knows God's will for you, so ask for help and Chamuel will sort the rest out.

Here are some examples of the mysterious ways in which Chamuel has helped people locate what they were seeking:

When Amanda Peart got a new handbag, she threw her old one in the garbage. Unfortunately, a couple of days later after she emptied her new purse completely, she realized that her iPod had been in the old bag, which had by now gone to the dump.

Very upset, Amanda asked Archangel Chamuel to help. The next day in the supermarket, she opened her new purse and was shocked to find her iPod. She says, "I know for absolute certain that the iPod hadn't been there previously because I had literally tipped everything out of my bag onto the floor in my desperation and annoyance that I'd lost it."

Amanda's story is typical of the Chamuel stories that I receive, in that the lost article reappears mysteriously. I do believe that the angels bring the item back to us once we've asked Chamuel to locate it.

You can also call upon Chamuel on behalf of another person, as Nicholas Davis discovered.

Nicholas's roommate owned very expensive sunglasses that he treasured because it had taken him a long time to find the right pair. Then one day he lost them! Nicholas and his roommate searched the entire house, but they were gone.

Then Nicholas recalled that Archangel Chamuel helps retrieve lost items, so with full faith he asked for the sunglasses to be returned to his friend.

The next day, Nicholas got up to get ready for work. He'd forgotten about the incident until he saw his roommate happily wearing his shades. Nicholas remarked, "I thought you lost those. Where'd you find them?"

His pal replied, "It's a miracle! My sunglasses were on the dining table when I got up this morning; and please don't ask me how or why they got there, because I can't give you an answer to any of your questions. They were just there!"

But Nicholas knew in his heart that Archangel Chamuel performed the miracle and *does* perform them every single day.

When you ask Chamuel to help find something, pay close attention to the thoughts, ideas, visions, and feelings you receive. That's because Chamuel is letting you know where to find the object through these means. He may tell you to look in a place that seems illogical because you've already looked there several times. But check anyway, because the angels may have brought it to that location.

Gillian and Gary Smalley love to teach people about Archangel Chamuel's amazing ability to find lost objects. They learned of this skill because Chamuel located their own missing items. The first time this occurred was when they'd misplaced an important cassette tape. After Gillian asked for Chamuel's guidance, she kept getting the thought to look in the garage on the second shelf of a storage rack. But she knew she'd already checked that shelf, so she dismissed the guidance . . . until a voice said to her, "Go and take another look." And when she did, the tape was there!

The second time was when the couple's business was threatened with a lawsuit, and they needed supporting records to back up their defense. Unfortunately, they'd tossed out all that paperwork a couple of years before. So Gillian said to Gary, "Nothing is lost in God's eyes, and therefore I'll ask Archangel Chamuel to find it for us."

When the couple visited Gary's brother and began talking about the pending lawsuit, their sister-in-law said, "Oh, by the way, look what I found— I don't know what we're doing with this." It was the paperwork that the Smalleys had thrown away!

Gillian and Gary were protected from the lawsuit, thanks to Chamuel.

Chamuel can help you find *anything,* as long as you're willing to listen and follow his guidance, as a man named Michael Muth discovered. When Michael needed his English-German dictionary, he automatically went to the place where he always kept it—but it wasn't there. So Michael searched the entire room, but still no dictionary. He then looked in the living room, in the kitchen, on the balcony, and in the bathroom.

Then Michael remembered that Archangel Chamuel helps us locate missing objects, so he decided to ask him for help. Within a few minutes, he got the answer as a "knowingness" that the dictionary was in his bedroom. And sure enough, it was!

Like a satellite, Chamuel can see everything on Earth. So, he's a wonderful companion to call upon if you feel lost or afraid. Chamuel will guide you safely to your destination, as Timothy's story illustrates.

When Timothy arrived in a strange town's train depot late at night, he wasn't sure where his hotel was located. There were no taxis, so he began walking. No one was around to give directions, and Timothy asked Archangel Chamuel to please guide him to the hotel.

Timothy just wandered after this, hoping to find someone to point him in the right direction. Imagine his surprise when he walked directly to the hotel without any detours or wrong turns. Not having the faintest idea which direction to go, Timothy had walked right to the front door of his destination!

Whether you're seeking your soul mate, a better job, or the location of your car keys, Chamuel can use his celestial vision to help. In our next chapter, we'll work with Archangel Ariel, who can help us connect more closely with nature.

Chapter Six

ARIEL

"Dear Archangel Ariel, please help me connect with the healing power and spirit of nature."

Ariel is also known as: Arael and Arieael

Ariel's name means: "The Lion or Lioness of God"

Archangel Ariel has appeared in Coptic, apocryphal, and mystical Judeo-Christian writings as both an overseer of nature and the regulator of the underworld. In the latter role, Ariel takes on the fierce presence of punishing those who transgress into darkness.

The association of Ariel with the spirit of nature was immortalized by Shakespeare, who portrayed this archangel as a tree sprite in *The Tempest*. In the

play, Ariel gains secret knowledge on behalf of the magician Prospero.

In the biblical chapter Isaiah, there's a reference to a Holy Land city named Ariel, which theologians believe is symbolic of Jerusalem, since it's said that King David dwelled there.

Ariel has appeared in artwork as a small female fairy to illustrate Shakespeare's *The Tempest* and as a delicate young effeminate angel in one of the Sopo Archangels paintings from 1600s Colombia. The Sopo painting is entitled "Ariel: Command of God," although it doesn't convey any fierceness.

The gender of this angel is controversial. Ultimately, it's not an important point compared to the vast resources Ariel offers us. Besides, Ariel, like the other angels, doesn't have a physical body, and so is essentially genderless or androgynous. However, her specialties and energy exude femininity to me, so I have always connected to Ariel as a feminine archangel.

Ariel is a healing angel who works closely with Archangel Raphael, especially when it comes to helping birds, fish, and other animals.

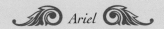

Environmental Life Purposes

"Thank you, Archangel Ariel, for guiding me toward the best way for me to help the earth's environment."

Archangel Ariel is believed to be a leader of the Virtues choir of angels—those who govern the order of the physical universe, watching over the sun, moon, stars, and all of the planets, including Earth. For this reason, Ariel is intimately involved in environmentalism. If you feel called to work in fields protective of the earth's ecology, oceans, air quality, or animals, then Ariel can help you.

When Susan* was a little girl, she had a natural connection with the environment. She even led her parents through each room in their house and coached them to replace toxic cleaning products and energy wasters with more eco-friendly alternatives. So it makes sense that now, as an adult, Susan has developed a relationship with the ecological angel, Archangel Ariel.

For example, Susan felt strongly guided by Ariel to continue her environmental work in a larger way. She didn't know how to do this, though, so she asked for support. Susan felt the archangel's reassurance as

---

*Name changed at her request.

an intuitive answer: *If I trusted in my angel team, everything I needed would be provided for me.*

Sure enough, Susan began seeing repetitive signs that told her she was to help with the restoration of her local park. Susan realized she was supposed to raise money for this cause, but didn't know how. So Ariel gave her specific signs and guidance to create a quilt project, where everyone could submit an eight-inch square that represented their personal connection to nature. Susan was guided to raffle this quilt on Earth Day (April 22 annually) and donate the proceeds toward the park's restoration. She followed this vision and her intuition and remains connected with Ariel on this and other environmental projects.

Manifestation of Supplies

"Dear Archangel Ariel, please help my family and me have the supplies and support that we need for our happy, healthy lives."

As the angel of our planet's natural resources, Ariel ensures the proper treatment of people and animals as part of her mission. So she works to ensure that there's enough healthful food, clean water, proper shelter, and other necessary supplies.

Therefore, you can ask Ariel to help you in meeting your earthly needs.

As Amy McRay was shuffling her *Archangel Oracle Cards,* the card of Archangel Ariel with the message "Prosperity" flew out. She fell asleep as she meditated upon the card's words and the beautiful image of Ariel holding a cornucopia. As she slept, Amy could see and feel Ariel showering her with a prosperous flow.

So Amy credited Ariel when she got the news the next day that she'd won a laptop computer from a contest she had forgotten she'd entered! And the interesting twist was that the contest was about going paperless, a very eco-friendly theme that Ariel would definitely endorse.

Connecting with Nature

"Thank you, Archangel Ariel, for being my guide to nature."

Ariel can also help you interact with nature comfortably and safely. She's a wonderful angel to call upon when you're hiking or camping, for example. And as a woman named Ann McWilliam discovered, Ariel can also help with barbecues!

Tiny insects were infesting Ann's barbecue as she grilled veggie burgers. She didn't want to use bug spray, so she instead called upon Archangel Ariel for help, since she's the nature archangel.

Ann said, "Archangel Ariel! Please help me find a way to get rid of these bugs without hurting them."

Within seconds, the thought *Vinegar* popped into Ann's head. She doubted the message for a minute, but it repeated itself. So Ann sprayed her grill with vinegar, and the bugs went away and have *stayed* away!

The archangel Ariel will also introduce you to the nonphysical side of nature as well, if you'll ask for her assistance. If you've always wanted to connect with the fairies or other elementals, seek out Ariel as your guide. She'll help you navigate through the nature-spirit realm so that you'll meet the benevolent beings who populate gardens, parks, flowers, trees, and bodies of water.

Ariel can also help heal wild or domesticated mammals, birds, and fish. Many times I've cradled an injured bird in my hands while asking for Ariel's help. Within minutes, the bird regains its life force and ability to fly.

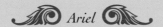

With her connection to nature and environmentalism, Archangel Ariel plays an important role in ensuring the health of our planet. In our next chapter, we'll connect with the profound and mystical archangel Metatron, who also helps us in important ways.

Chapter Seven

METATRON

*"Dear Archangel Metatron, please help me
deepen my connection to God and guide me to feel
and understand the profound love of the Divine."*

Metatron is one of two archangels whose names
don't end in the *-el* suffix, which means "of God."
That's because Metatron and Sandalphon were both
human prophets who lived such pious lives that they
were rewarded with ascension into the archangel
realm.

There's no consensus on the origin of the name
Metatron, nor are there records of him being called
anything else. The Talmud, the Zohar, and the apoc-
ryphal Book of Enoch do refer to Metatron as the
"Lesser YHVH" (*YHVH* are the Hebrew letters for
God) and make reference to Metatron sitting as a

scribe next to God. Some rabbis believe that in Exodus when God says to obey the angel who is leading the mass departure "since my Name is in him," this refers to Metatron.

Although Metatron isn't named in the canonical Bible, the ascension of Enoch (who belonged to the seventh generation after Adam, was a son of Jared, and was a great-great-grandfather to Noah) is described in Genesis. There it states that the 365-year-old Enoch walked with God; then he was no more because God took him away. Later in Hebrews, it is said that Enoch didn't experience death, and his body couldn't be found because God had taken him away.

The mystical Judaic book the Zohar describes Metatron as "the highest archangel, esteemed more than any other of God's hosts." It says that Metatron rules over all, the living things below and the living things above, and is the mediator between Heaven and Earth.

Metatron's Cube

"Thank you, Archangel Metatron, for utilizing your healing cube to purify the energy of my body, mind, and emotions."

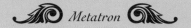

Metatron is associated with the *Merkabah,* which is described in the Torah's Ezekiel as the chariot of God. The chariot itself is made of angels, and Seraphim power the vehicle with their flashes of light. In the Book of Enoch, Metatron is given charge over the Merkabah. It's also said that the Sephiroth Tree of Life in the Kabbalah is a Merkabah chariot for the spiritual path. Metatron presides over the first sphere of the Sephiroth.

Today, the association of Metatron and the Merkabah delves into "sacred geometry." The vehicle of the Merkabah is now depicted as a compilation of the Platonic solids, which represent the basis of all physical matter. We call this "Metatron's Cube" or the "Flower of Life."

Archangel Metatron utilizes the Merkabah cube for healing and clearing away lower energies. The cube spins clockwise and uses centrifugal force to push away unwanted energy residue. You can call upon Metatron and his healing cube to clear you. His aura coloring is deep pink and dark green.

As a sensitive lightworker, Sue Tanida absorbs emotional and physical energies from people around her. They affect her mood and energy levels, and she's so busy with her career that she doesn't always have time to meditate and realign her own energies.

So Sue was relieved to discover that calling on Archangel Metatron proved to be a huge help! She simply says, "Please, Metatron, use your cube to re-align my energy and remove from me that which does not belong to me or serve me."

Sue feels and clairvoyantly sees Metatron using his "cube" like a plumbing snake to unblock her energy lines. The cube goes energetically through the crown of Sue's head and down through her body along the spine, and comes up carrying any sludge she's absorbed. Then the archangel purifies this lower energy, and Sue is refreshed and revived.

Like Sue, Natalia Kuna recently learned that she could quickly clear her body's energy centers by calling upon Archangel Metatron, so she decided to try

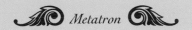
this one day. First Natalia relaxed and thought of Metatron, mentally asking him to clear her chakras.

Natalia immediately felt Metatron hand her a round energy ball, and she intuitively knew to use her hands to glide it over each chakra. As she did so, she could feel the energy rise and change over them. She especially felt a distinct buzzing energy and warmth as the ball reached her heart chakra, dissolving away old pain.

Natalia was overjoyed by the experience, as it not only cleared and healed her chakras, body, and mind, but it also boosted her confidence in trusting her intuition—something she'd been praying for.

As the scribe of God, Metatron, with his sacred geometry, is a teacher of esoteric knowledge. If you're trying to grasp high-level concepts, Archangel Metatron and Archangel Raziel (whom you'll meet in Chapter 12) are wonderful teachers to call upon.

For example, psychotherapist Sandra Guassi realized that she'd reached the limits of what psychology could teach her about life and the universe. So she began studying mystical topics such as numerology, astrology, and ancient esoteric wisdom.

Soon after, Sandra meditated upon connecting with her guardian angel. She silently asked the angel's name and clearly heard "Metatron." The name

resonated with her so strongly that she got goose bumps all over her body. The energy of this connection was so powerful that Sandra began crying tears of joy.

As soon as she opened her eyes from the meditation, Sandra began questioning the validity of the message, wondering whether Metatron was really with her. This question was met with guidance, in which she was encouraged to do numerology using the name of Metatron, comparing it with that of her own name. She was awestruck to find that *her* name and Metatron's contained the same numerological path. This helped Sandra accept the reality that this archangel was her guardian. Since that time, Sandra has become an Angel Therapist, and she has developed a close bond with Metatron and other angels.

Archangel Metatron has insights into the malleability of the physical universe, which is actually composed of atoms and thought energy. He can help you work with universal energies for healing, understanding, teaching, and even bending time.

Amy McRae has learned to trust Archangel Metatron to get her to her appointments on time. She knows from experience that he can bend time and space. Even when Amy knows she's going to be late, somehow Metatron gets her to her destination

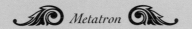

promptly—without speeding, and usually with extra time to spare. Amy has had such success in time management with Archangel Metatron that her father is now calling the angel "Saint Timex"!

The Angel of Highly Sensitive Children

"Dear Archangel Metatron, please watch over my children and guide me as to the best way to help them develop and maintain their spiritual gifts."

Archangel Metatron teaches esoteric wisdom to children and adults. He seems to take a special interest in highly sensitive young people who are misunderstood or even medicated because their spiritual gifts make them socially awkward.

If you or your child need assistance in adjusting to socialization at school, work, or home, Metatron can help. As an example, Melanie Orders has two daughters who are very sensitive to energies, chemicals, and anything harsh. Ten-year-old Serene has difficulty being around loud noises or any form of anger or violence. Just seeing an image of war on television briefly caused her to have a sleepless night. Melanie and her husband hadn't even realized that Serene had seen the violent image on TV, as

it had only flashed on for a moment during channel changing when she was walking by. But when she couldn't sleep and kept crying, the girl admitted the source of her distress: "Mommy, I can't stop seeing the man on TV!"

So Melanie called upon Archangel Metatron, as the overseer of sensitive children, for help. As she closed her eyes, she saw a vision of a large angel standing in front of Serene. Metatron began soothing Serene's thoughts, helping her release the violent image from her mind. Soon the girl said she felt better and was able to go to sleep by herself.

Melanie frequently calls upon Metatron to help with her children so that they'll stay sensitive but still live in harmony with the present world's sometimes-harsh energies. She and her husband are even more aware of their children's sensitivities now, and no one in the household watches the news on television anymore.

Melanie's work with Archangel Metatron truly illustrates his mission to help sensitive and psychic children get along in the material world.

Sometimes highly sensitive children are restless and suffer from insomnia. At 4 in the morning, Orietta Mammarella's toddler Jasmina was restless and was keeping her parents awake. She pulled on her daddy's

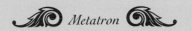

ears, sang songs, and played. Frustrated and tired, Orietta appealed to Archangel Metatron for help.

She heard "angel whispers" in her ear to indicate that Jasmina needed to go back into her own bed. Metatron counseled Orietta that the little girl was testing her parents' boundaries. So Orietta put Jasmina in her bed and asked Metatron to please help everyone rest comfortably. And it worked! Jasmina slept until 9 A.M., giving the household a wonderful opportunity to sleep in.

Orietta works with Metatron frequently now and refers to the archangel as the "Super Nanny."

Archangel Metatron not only helps with the parenting of acutely sensitive children, but he also aids in conception and pregnancy, as Claire Timmis discovered. Claire connects with Archangel Metatron whenever she's near water. She perceives Metatron's energy as a very high frequency, beyond what we can perceive with our human senses. To Claire, his energy is powerful yet gentle, and his guidance is firm and strong. She has noticed that most of the archangels offer love but then back away from giving guidance that could be perceived as controlling. Metatron, on the other hand—while not controlling—is very clear about his advice.

When Claire was showering one day, she had a vision of the archangel telling her that she'd soon

conceive a gentle child. A few weeks later, she discovered she was pregnant. Her entire pregnancy was a profound spiritual experience, and she has felt Metatron's presence and support during every aspect of motherhood. Claire says, "Archangel Metatron helps me make the world a brighter place through my own actions and those I teach to my children."

Life Purpose Involving Working with Highly Sensitive Children

"Thank you, Archangel Metatron, for guiding and supporting my career as a healer and teacher who helps highly sensitive children."

If you feel drawn to help children, especially acutely sensitive and psychic young people, then Archangel Metatron can mentor you in your career. He knows which child-related field you'd find most meaningful; and if you ask, he'll guide your education and job search and bring work and clients to you.

For example, the Angel Therapist Kristy Ayala (who was aided by Gabriel in her spiritual calling in the story in Chapter 3) received clear guidance from Archangel Metatron during her meditations. She

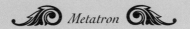

was in the process of moving away from conducting traditional psychotherapy. Each time she asked for guidance about her true life purpose, Archangel Metatron would appear to Kristy. He showed her that her purpose involved working with highly sensitive children, who are often referred to as *Indigo, Crystal,* and *Rainbow* children.

Kristy's visions were quite specific. The archangel showed her that she'd be guided step-by-step in the moment with these children and their parents. She says, "He showed me that I'd be conducting one-on-one counseling sessions, with an emphasis on understanding and connecting with their spiritual path." Metatron also revealed to Kristy that she'd be teaching classes for children, parents, and caregivers about working with angels.

Well, Metatron's visions and guidance have all come true for Kristy, and the classes are going very well. Kristy says, "Working with Archangel Metatron has allowed me to receive the information needed to customize sessions for each family based on what they need. I have found Archangel Metatron to be very supportive, loving, and dedicated to these families and to me as I continue to serve."

Although Archangel Metatron is a high-level being, he is very accessible to us all because of his dedication to teaching the practical application of esoteric wisdom. He also deeply cares about highly sensitive people.

In our next chapter, we'll connect with Archangel Sandalphon, who's been referred to as Metatron's brother, since they both followed similar paths from prophets to archangeldom.

Chapter Eight

SANDALPHON

*"Dear Archangel Sandalphon, please deliver my prayer
to Heaven, that it may be heard and answered."*

Sandalphon is also known as: Ophan or Sal-
dolfon

Sandalphon's name means: "Brother" or
"Brother Together"

Like Metatron, Sandalphon's name ends in *-on*
instead of *-el*, signifying his origin as a human
prophet. Sandalphon was the biblical prophet Elijah,
who ascended at the end of his human life, just as
Metratron did. Interestingly, Metatron presides over
the entrance to the spheres of the Kabbalah's Tree of
Life, and Sandalphon presides over its exit.

In Sandalphon's human existence, Elijah was the one Jesus was compared to when he asked his disciples, "Who do the people say I am?" This may be because Elijah was said to be a precursor of the coming Messiah.

The functions associated with Sandalphon include being an intercessor for prayers between humans and God, helping determine the gender of a coming child, and acting as a patron to musicians. The Talmud and the Kabbalah describe Sandalphon as a deliverer of prayers from Earth to Heaven. This may be because of his legendary height, which is said to *span* from Heaven to Earth.

In the Kabbalah, the last Sephirah of the Tree of Life is called *Malkuth,* which refers to the entrance to metaphysical knowledge of humankind. Archangel Sandalphon presides over the Malkuth, the culmination of spiritual experience and knowledge funneling into the physical world.

In other words, Sandalphon takes the esoteric and puts it into practical application as he delivers and answers prayers.

As an example, when Jenn Prothero sold her house, she didn't know where she'd move. All she knew was that she wanted to escape city life and that the angels would guide her to a perfect place. She

meditated every day and asked the angels for assistance in finding her new home.

Jenn looked at a few places, but nothing felt right. She also had a fast-approaching deadline to move out of her house so that the new owners could move in.

So Jenn called upon Archangel Sandalphon, the angel who delivers prayers to, and answers from, God. She said to Sandalphon, "Please go to God and ask Him for the answers I'm seeking." The next morning during meditation, she heard a soft voice say, "McNaughton Street." Jenn knew she'd received the guidance she'd been seeking, so she called her real-estate agent.

Sure enough, there was a perfect home for sale on McNaughton Street, and Jenn signed the sales papers the following evening.

The Angel of Music

"Dear Archangel Sandalphon, I ask that you channel the harmonious and healing music of the spheres through my voice and instruments."

Sandalphon works with the angels who continually sing praises to God, creating celestial music that provides protection for us all. Some theologians consider Sandalphon either to be a *hazan* (Hebrew for a master musician) or to be the patron of people who are hazans.

Either way, many musicians have benefited from calling upon Archangel Sandalphon for musical help. I frequently ask him to assist my guitar playing, or when I'm learning a new song (especially a challenging one).

Songwriter and singer Anna Taylor was working on the tracks for her debut album, *Already Here,* when her producer asked if she planned on including a song about angels. After all, she was an Angel Therapist, the producer pointed out.

Yet Anna was reluctant to compose a song about angels, since so many fine ones on the topic already existed. Still, at the encouragement of her producer, she decided to call upon the angel of music, Archangel Sandalphon, for inspiration and support. Within seconds of making this request, Anna got her help!

Anna opened her laptop and began typing words to her song, as if she were taking dictation from Sandalphon. Then she looked up and saw a flash of soft turquoise light, which is the color of the music angel's aura. When she was finished, Anna realized that she'd penned a song that encompassed everything she'd wanted to say about angels.

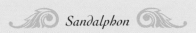

Anna says, "I feel Sandalphon's powerful energy right in front of me when I sing this song, and every so often I'll catch a glimpse of his beautiful turquoise halo color, as if he's saying hello." Anna now requests Sandalphon's help for everything associated with her music and singing.

Sandalphon's gracious and powerfully gentle presence can support you in developing a closer connection to God and your spirituality. He will help you feel the love of the Divine and the security of knowing that you are watched over and cared for. In the next chapter, we'll connect with the Archangel Azrael, who supports us through endings and transitions.

Chapter Nine

AZRAEL

*"Dear Archangel Azrael, please heal my
heart and help me move on in my life."*

Azrael is also known as: Ezraeil, Izrail, Izrael, or
Mala al-Maut

His name means: "Whom God helps"

Azrael is the "angel of death," in the most beautiful and healing sense of the word. This is a far cry from
the morbid image of a grim reaper stealing people
away. Azrael, in contrast, is a grief counselor who
lovingly guides souls to Heaven after their crossing.
He then consoles the survivors and helps them heal
from grief.

Islamic theology holds that Azrael carries out God's will for the souls of the deceased with profound reverence.

Azrael is sometimes confused with the similar-sounding name Azazael, who is considered a demon or fallen angel. Yet their personas, missions, and energies couldn't be more different. Our Azrael is a pure and trustworthy being of God's light.

Healing for the Grief Stricken

Azrael helps with all aspects of loss, death, and transitions. If your heart is heavy with grief, call upon Azrael for healing and support, as Carmen Carignan did.

The holiday season had been difficult for Carmen since her mother's recent passing. Carmen missed her mom terribly, especially since her birthday was so near to Christmas. It had been a while since Carmen had sensed her mother's spiritual presence or received a dream visitation from her.

So Carmen turned to Archangel Azrael for comfort and support during the holidays. She asked Azrael to send her a sign that her mother was okay and nearby.

Well, Carmen got her sign on Christmas Eve when she and her family unwrapped gifts next to the holiday tree. After all the presents had been opened, Carmen's brother handed her a gift box. As she unwrapped it, a familiar fragrance permeated her nostrils. It was her mother's embroidered turquoise cosmetics kit!

Carmen cradled the contents after she unzipped the kit, as each half-used bottle of perfume and lotion was filled with her mother's energy and presence. Carmen's brother explained that he'd found the kit in his house, with no idea how it had gotten there. He just knew that he had to give it to Carmen.

She says:

> My heart just swelled, and tears began to flow as I came to the realization that this had all been Divinely orchestrated by Archangel Azrael as a sign that my mother was okay, just like I had asked. This truly was the most beautiful Christmas present I had ever received, as it brought me so much peace and tranquility within my being.

Loss can take many forms, and grief is the normal reaction to any kind of ending. Fortunately, Archangel Azrael is there to catch us whenever we fall, as Claudio Moreno experienced after he and his girlfriend broke up.

In fact, Claudio first connected with Archangel Azrael when the woman he loved left him without explanation. He prayed for spiritual help, both to effect a reconciliation and to feel better. But deep down, he admitted to himself that he wanted to remain sad and feel sorry for himself.

One night while grieving over his relationship, Claudio randomly opened to a page in the book *Archangels & Ascended Masters* and read about Archangel Azrael. Unfamiliar with the angel, Claudio read the invocation on the page and let the matter go.

A couple days later, Claudio's mother sent him an interesting article about Teotihuacán, Mexico. This sounded like a wonderful healing vacation destination, so Claudio contacted a friend named Hector in Mexico, who just "happened" to be conducting a guided trip through Teotihuacán and other Mexican towns that month. Knowing this was a clear sign, Claudio went to Mexico to join Hector's tour.

On the trip, Hector began spontaneously discussing the angel of death, which Claudio later learned was the role of Archangel Azrael. That evening, Claudio had another sign of Azrael's presence when he opened a John Irving novel and read another reference to the angel of death.

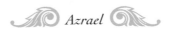

Claudio wondered what these signs meant. He could feel the angels' presence, helping him overcome grief about his relationship. But he couldn't hear their messages. The next day Claudio, Hector, and the rest of the group visited Teotihuacán and walked "the path of the dead" arm in arm.

During this walking meditation, Claudio saw a mental vision of a blond man with huge white wings wearing pale burgundy-colored armor and a light helmet. Claudio found him very intense and beautiful.

Silently, Claudio said, *I know you're Azrael, the angel of death, and I know that you're here to help me.* Claudio noticed that the angel held a huge spear, and he mentally appealed to Azrael to use his spear to cut away his painful thoughts and feelings. Claudio felt much better, as he sensed Azrael healing his heart of relationship grief.

Claudio continued communing with Azrael after he returned home. The messages and help that the archangel had for him were firm and clear. Claudio summarizes:

> Azrael let me know that I was responsible for creating this hell I was living in. It was my doing, nobody else's, and he reminded me that I shouldn't blame others for my

feelings. He also made me understand that by empowering fear and bad feelings, I was hurting not only myself, but I was collaborating in making the world a worse place. Azrael also wanted me to know that he loves releasing people from fear. He wanted me to know that whenever I empowered him, he would go into the depths of my own personal hell and rescue me. He has done so for me many times since then, and he now helps me prevent my mind from creating ideas that will harm my emotional body.

Claudio learned from Azrael that the battlefield of love versus fear was only in his mind and nowhere else. Azrael taught him that the only choice that truly matters is whether we align ourselves with love. Claudio appreciated Azrael's practical and logical teachings, and he used them to heal his heart and mind and find a newfound sense of happiness.

Support for Grief Counselors

In addition to the grief stricken, Archangel Azrael helps those who perform grief counseling. At your request, Azrael can guide your speech as you talk to a

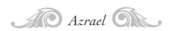

bereaved person so that you choose comforting words. Azrael can also help you deliver a beautiful eulogy.

If you're a professional counselor, then you know how often unhealed grief morphs into emotional and relationship issues, addictions, and other psychological maladies. So it's a good idea to invite Azrael into your healing practice.

During one 12-month period, three of therapist Kristy Ayala's close family members passed away. There wasn't much time to grieve for one loved one before another passing would take place. Kristy had support from her husband, fortunately, and the comforting help of Archangel Azrael.

As Kristy began to heal from the grief, Azrael showed her that she'd be returning the same sort of support to others who were newly grieving. The archangel explained that Kristy would be conducting mediumship sessions to connect her counseling clients with their departed loved ones.

At first Kristy worried that her clients' despair would be too intense for her, since she was still overcoming grief herself. But Azrael assured her that he'd be present for all sessions to support everyone involved. Upon hearing that, Kristy moved forward with her mediumship work, and now she finds this type of session to be her favorite healing modality.

Azrael continues to support Kristy's personal and professional grief work and mediumship sessions, especially when she or her clients need comfort.

Archangel Azrael holds our hands and steadies us through the transitions of life. He helps us acknowledge, and deal with the fact, that endings and beginnings are natural. In the next chapter, we'll connect with the archangel Jophiel, who shows us how to create a beautiful life.

Chapter Ten

JOPHIEL

*"Dear Archangel Jophiel, thank you for helping
me beautify my thoughts and my life."*

Jophiel is also known as: Iofiel, Iophiel, Za-
phiel, or Zophiel

Jophiel's name means: "Beauty of God"

Jophiel is listed as one of the seven principal
archangels in Pseudo-Dionysius's *De Coelesti Hierar-
chia* ("Celestial Hierarchy"), a 5th-century work on
angelology that has been influential in Christian
theology. It's said that this work influenced Thomas
Aquinas's writings about the nine choirs of angels.

As the angel of beauty, Jophiel has a distinctly feminine energy. Her mission is to bring beauty to all aspects of life, including:

- **Thoughts:** Helping you hold more positive viewpoints about your life, relationships, and circumstances

- **Feelings:** Filling your heart with warm feelings of gratitude and enjoyment

- **Home and office:** Helping you reduce clutter and create a meaningful environment that's conducive to work and relaxation

- **Personal self:** Guiding you in all aspects of self-care, including beautifying yourself

Archangel Jophiel can help you quickly shift from a negative to a positive mind-set. She's also wonderful to call upon to heal misunderstandings with other people. Jophiel casts a wide net with her ability to bring beauty to your life, including helping with hair, makeup, and wardrobe.

Sometimes people worry about "bothering" angels with trivial concerns because they believe that their request pulls them away from more pressing matters. Yet, as I've said, angels are unlimited beings who can help unlimited numbers of people and situations simultaneously. They would like to get more involved with our lives, the small and the big aspects, to help us experience peace at every moment.

For example, when Karen Forrest was scheduled to appear on television to promote her book (a story that appeared in Chapter 3), her sister Lesa asked what she planned to wear. Karen responded that she hadn't quite figured that out yet. Lesa looked completely alarmed that with only hours to go before the TV appearance, Karen didn't have an outfit selected.

Karen reassured her sister that Archangel Jophiel was handling her wardrobe. After all, she had helped her with shopping and dressing in the past. Then Karen asked Archangel Jophiel to guide her wardrobe selections. When it was time to get dressed, she called upon the archangel again.

Immediately, Karen relaxed and saw a mental image of a short-sleeved gray blouse. When she tried it on, she realized that it looked great and completely suited her body posture while sitting for an interview.

Like Karen, I've also called upon Jophiel to help me select outfits for my workshops. Lest you think beautifying or shopping too trivial for a sacred archangel, keep in mind that Jophiel and the other angels are enacting God's will of peace on Earth. So it is the angels' sacred honor to help us with whatever brings us peace.

Maria de los Angeles Duong has learned from experience what a wonderful shopping companion the archangel Jophiel is. Far from trivializing this powerful angel's functions, calling upon Jophiel is something you can do *anytime* you want to beautify your life . . . and that includes purchasing aesthetically pleasing clothing, furniture, or other items.

Maria had been searching for a purple scarf and sweater and black flat ballet shoes for some time, without luck. The shoes in particular were eluding Maria, as they seemed to be sold out in her size everywhere she checked.

Then she recalled that Jophiel, the angel of beauty, could help her locate beautiful and affordable clothing. So Maria asked her to lead her to these items. Immediately, she was guided to drive to a small shopping mall where she rarely went. Maria was only mildly surprised that her previously hard-to-find shoes and sweater were right there, in her size and on sale!

With much appreciation, Maria thanked Jophiel for this help. Next, the archangel guided her to a

shop where she found two beautiful purple scarves. But she wondered which one she should purchase.

Jophiel must have sent Earth angels to help, because a moment later, another shopper remarked that the bright purple scarf in Maria's hand was much prettier than the other one. Happy with her purchase, Maria wore the scarf on the remainder of her shopping trip and received two other lovely compliments on its color. Maria says, "Thank you, beautiful Archangel Jophiel!"

The Feng Shui Angel

When you ask Jophiel to help you beautify your life, you may feel compelled to start donating or selling unwanted items. I affectionately and respectfully refer to Jophiel as the "Feng Shui Angel," after the ancient Asian art of room arrangement. Jophiel knows how much an organized environment affects our energy levels, mood, sleep patterns, and even health.

Jophiel's halo color is deep fuchsia, so if you begin to see flashes or sparkles of hot pink light or if you're suddenly attracted to this color, it's a sign that this archangel is with you.

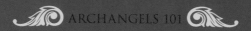
Jophiel reminds us of the joy of beauty and helps us live happier lives as a result. In the next chapter, we'll meet the radiant archangel Haniel.

Chapter Eleven

HANIEL

"Dear Archangel Haniel, thank you for helping me gracefully accept and appreciate myself, others, and my life."

Haniel is also known as: Aniel, Hanael, or Hanniel

Haniel's name means: "The Grace of God"

In the Kabbalah, Haniel presides over the seventh, or *Netzach,* Sephirah (emanation of God's will). This sphere is related to victory and represents our inner world of intuition, imagination, and emotions.

The Netzach Sephirah marks the beginning of humans' free will, and the expression of endurance and tenacity. It is the embodiment of earthly love.

As with the Netzach's exploration of intuition and imagination, the archangel Haniel radiates inner qualities outwardly like the full moon. Mysterious and feminine, Haniel has been revered since the Babylonian era, which tied astronomy into religion.

Archangel Haniel can help you develop your intuition and clairvoyance, as well as any aspect of sacred feminine energy. She is, in essence, a goddess-like archangel, but is not to be confused with the angel of the planet Venus, Anael. Haniel is the angel of the moon, particularly the full moon, akin to a lunar deity. Still, she remains a monotheistic angel faithful to the will and worship of God.

Women's Emotional and Physical Health Issues

It's very effective to call upon Haniel during the full moon, especially if there's anything you'd like to release or heal. Haniel can particularly help with women's issues.

Natalie Yates has worked with Archangel Haniel for quite a few years now. She finds Haniel's energy to be gently nurturing, with a particular sort of kindness to it. Since Haniel is associated with the moon, Natalie often calls upon the archangel during the full moon to release any negativity. She sits outside beneath it and says, "I ask Archangel Haniel and the energy of the full moon to please help me release [naming whatever it is]."

Within moments, Natalie experiences a rush of energy that feels like a sweeping motion washing over her. She can practically see Haniel's wings fluttering over her, removing the residue of the energy that she's releasing.

Natalie has also had great success in asking for Haniel's help in relieving menstrual pain. She says that when she first began asking Haniel for help with period-related discomfort, the relief would take a while. But the more she works with Haniel, the faster the assistance arrives each month. Natalie has also been guided to place a moonstone crystal pendant in the full moonlight to "charge it up with healing energy" and wear this during her menstrual periods.

Natalie calls upon Archangel Haniel during full moons for help in releasing old patterns and negativity. She says that when she's outside in the moonlight and calling upon Haniel, her body is covered from head to toe in "angel tingles" as she physically feels the powerful healing energy of the archangel sweeping over her. Afterward, she feels refreshed and so much lighter, thanks to Haniel and the full moon.

Of course, you can call upon Haniel anytime, not just during the full moon. She has a soft, sweet feminine presence that's also regal. She reminds me of a magical princess.

In addition, Haniel is a compassionate healer of heartbreak and other emotional pain.

As an example, Jessica Welsh felt upset by a painful love relationship in which she and her partner never seemed to connect. So she meditated and asked the angels to help her heal. Jessica saw and felt Haniel very clearly. The archangel waved her hands over Jessica's body, stopping at each chakra to pull out lower energies. She then enveloped her in white light. Archangel Raphael also briefly joined Haniel to surround Jessica in healing green light. When Raphael left, Haniel announced to Jessica, "You are now healed."

Jessica recalls that after that healing session with Haniel and Raphael, she felt better than she ever had in her entire life. Since that session, Jessica no longer feels sadness about the relationship or holds anger toward her ex-partner. She has truly moved on!

Intuitive Support

As the expression of the inner world of intuition, Archangel Haniel is a supportive guide for those who wish to develop their spiritual gifts, like clairvoyance. Her bluish white halo color reminds me of the moon, and wearing moonstone can both amplify intuitive transmissions and also help you feel connected to Haniel.

Men as well as women can benefit from connecting to this archangel, as men also have feminine energy (just like women have male energy). Haniel can help members of both sexes awaken and trust their inner guidance.

Archangel Haniel helps us access the rich sources of wisdom we carry within ourselves and have clearer communications with the Divine. In this next chapter, we'll connect with another mystical and magical archangel: Raziel.

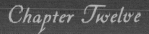

Chapter Twelve

RAZIEL

*"Dear Archangel Raziel, thank you for
guiding my spiritual understanding to
a place of knowingness and wisdom."*

Raziel is also known as: Ratziel

Raziel's name means: "The secrets of God"

Legend holds that the archangel Raziel sits so
close to the throne of God that he hears and writes
down everything God says. Raziel compiled this
knowledge into a book called *Sefer Raziel HaMalach*,
or the "Book of Raziel the Angel." This work is said
to contain all universal wisdom, and Raziel gave a
copy to Adam, the first man. Legend also holds that

it helped Noah gain the wisdom to build his ark. The book was passed down through the generations until it reached King Solomon. A modern pseudo-version of the work with the same title is presently available in bookstores.

Raziel (as Ratziel) is the archangel of the *Chokmah*, second Sephirah (aspect of God) of the Kabbalah's Tree of Life. There Raziel presides over the action of turning knowledge into practical wisdom. Raziel helps us humans ply our knowledge until it becomes spiritualized and second nature to us. In the Chokmah sphere, we learn how to stay focused and avoid tempting distractions. This requires attuning to our higher self, which is the connection to Divine wisdom.

Raziel's persona is similar to a wise old wizard. Think Merlin with huge eagle wings and you'll get a sense of Raziel's energy. This magical archangel is happy to impart esoteric wisdom, especially with a healing intention. His halo is rainbow hued, like sunlight reflecting through a clear quartz prism.

The Wisdom of Other Lifetimes

"Thank you, Archangel Raziel, for helping me heal away any fears from previous lifetimes so that I may focus clearly upon my present-day Divine life mission."

As the record keeper of ancient wisdom and secrets, Archangel Raziel sees each person's book of life or Akashic records, which includes soul contracts and past lifetimes. You don't need to believe in reincarnation, though, to benefit from experiencing Raziel's past-life healing work.

Raziel helps you recall all of the lessons that your soul has accumulated over time and condense these into usable energy for your present life's mission. Raziel also assists in healing from painful memories and past traumas, especially if they create fears of moving forward with your life mission. Additionally, Raziel can help you dissolve any troublesome vows you may have made in previous lifetimes, such as those of poverty, self-sacrifice, or chastity. If you don't want the effects of those vows in your present life, call upon Raziel to undo them by saying:

"Dear Archangel Raziel, I am willing to sever all vows of poverty, self-sacrifice, and chastity; and I ask that you help undo all effects of these vows in all directions of time for everyone concerned."

This prayer will normally undo any recurring negative patterns surrounding money and romance, and will usually result in increased self-esteem and feelings of self-worth.

Past-life work has been shown in studies to reduce or eliminate addictions and phobias, to increase feelings of happiness, and to help with relationships.

For example, Tia Spanelli has always been romantically attracted to men with dark hair, blue eyes, fair skin, and a foreign accent. However, there weren't any guys matching this description where Tia grew up. She says, "It was as if I made this 'dream guy' up in my imagination." Simultaneously, Tia had a strong fear of men taking sexual advantage of her, which had no basis in her experience since she'd never been abused in any way. In addition, Tia became a Francophile, studying everything about the French. She had no idea where these interests and phobias stemmed from.

Tia's questions were answered as she listened to my podcast recording about Archangel Raziel. She recalls what happened next:

> My eyes were rolling toward the back of my head at an uncontrollable speed, as if I were going back in time. After that, I was no longer at my desk, but was transported to Africa. I'm not sure which time period or which region, but I was in a village during what seemed to be an early part of the modern era.

I was a village girl—slender, with smooth mahogany skin and short hair. I wore a bracelet on my right arm. My dress was a tan color, with a thin sash around the waist, and resembled a cute cocktail dress. The man I had fallen in love with was a solider in the French army. He wasn't too tall, but a little taller than I was. His uniform was blue, which matched his sapphire eyes.

Our love was intense but ended as quickly as it began, after one of his soldier buddies followed him back to the village to our lovers' meeting place. The soldier revealed our location and situation to his officers, which meant an end to our relationship. I was captured and violated in many ways, resulting in my untimely death.

After that vision, I "woke up" and was back at my desk. So many feelings rushed through me, and there were tears in my eyes. But now I know why, from a very early age, I preferred a certain type of man, why I chose to take up French in high school and college over other languages, and why I was terribly afraid of being violated when I had no reason to be.

Tia has now moved on with her life, thanks to this insight and personal knowledge.

The Secrets of the Universe

"Dear Archangel Raziel, I ask that you teach me about God, universal wisdom, and the secrets of the universe, especially as they apply to living a more peaceful life."

As the archangel of secrets, esoteric information, and wisdom, Raziel is a natural teacher. Therefore, you can ask him any question, just as you would a mentor.

Tanya Snyman has had positive results when asking Archangel Raziel questions. She received very clear guidance when she recently wrote to him: "What does my future hold?" Tanya then wrote down the thoughts and feelings she received as answers from Raziel:

You are headed on your path. There is no direction. No right way or wrong way. You are just here, on your path. This is where you need to be. There is nothing else you need to know or remember. Except to just "be" on your path. All

will unfold according to Divine plan and timing. You need not concern yourself with this right now. Right now you are at peace. Right now you know everything there is to know. Right now is life. Right now is important.

This is the dearest and greatest gift of life. To live in the present. To be in the present. The present is where all the opportunities and gateways to life and love open up. Feel this feeling in your heart. This strong, knowing, loving feeling. This feeling that keeps you here now. It is helping you do work on this planet.

Archangel Raziel awakens our knowledge of our past and the esoteric wisdom of the universe. Next, we'll meet Archangel Raguel, who helps us put this healing wisdom into practice in our present-day relationships.

Chapter Thirteen

RAGUEL

"Dear Archangel Raguel, thank you for harmonizing all of my relationships and helping me to be a good friend to myself and all others."

Raguel is also known as: Raguil, Rasuil, Reuel, Ruhiel, Ruagel, or Ruahel

Raguel's name means: "Friend of God"

Archangel Raguel is primarily discussed in the apocryphal Book of Enoch and is listed as one of the seven principal archangels. Raguel is considered to be the archangel of orderliness, fairness, harmony, and justice. He also manages the relationships between angels and humans. In Enoch, Raguel dispensed justice to those who violated God's will.

The Archangel of Relationship Harmony

"Thank you, Archangel Raguel, for healing my relationship with [name of person] *and helping us both let go, forgive, and have compassion for the other person's point of view."*

As the "friend of God" meaning of his name implies, Raguel is the angel to turn to for harmonious relationships. He brings forgiveness, peace, and calm between people and heals misunderstandings. He can also help you attract wonderful friends who treat you with respect and integrity. Over the years, I've heard many stories where Raguel helped miraculously heal feuds.

For example, every night as she's falling asleep, a woman named Stevie says to Archangel Raguel, "Please heal any of my relationships that need healing and strengthen those that are important to me." This request came to fruition very recently when she and her close friend had an argument. Stevie's friend even stopped speaking to her!

Stevie didn't know how to heal the situation, so she asked Archangel Raguel to harmonize the relationship and bring its purpose to the surface so that she and her friend could resolve the issue. The next day, Stevie felt a reduction in tension between the two of them. They were able to have an honest talk and resolve the misunderstanding, and now their relationship is more solid than ever.

Archangel Raguel brings harmony to all relationships, including those of friendship, romance, family, and business. Sometimes he'll instantly heal the relationship, and other times he'll send intuitive guidance to you. You'll recognize this guidance as repetitive gut feelings, thoughts, visions, or signs that lead you to take healthful action steps in your relationships.

When Maria de los Angeles Duong (who was also mentioned in Chapter 10) and her husband were struggling with infertility issues, their marriage was filled with tension. So Maria began calling upon Archangel Raguel to smooth out their relationship. She immediately noticed that she and her husband were more understanding of one another. With Raguel's help, they were able to resolve their problems in more peaceful ways that were fair for both of them.

Little did Maria realize that Raguel would continue to help her personally.

When she recently had a positive pregnancy-test result, she was overjoyed! Unfortunately, she miscarried within days. Maria was distraught!

To help her heart and body heal, Maria booked a session with an intuitive bodyworker. During the session, the healer said, "I see a male angel. He says his name is Raguel, the Angel of Hope, and he's with you right now." The healer asked her if she'd ever heard of an angel named Raguel, and Maria knew that the angel was helping her retain hope that someday she and her husband would have a baby.

Archangel Raguel can help you with all aspects of your relationships, including the one with *yourself*. The next chapter features the archangel Jeremiel, who also shines healing light upon your inner self.

Chapter Fourteen

JEREMIEL

*"Dear Archangel Jeremiel, thank you for helping me
have clear spiritual visions of the Divine guidance that
will best lead me along the path of my life's purpose."*

Jeremiel is also known as: Eremiel, Ramiel, Remiel, or Jerahmeel

Jeremiel's name means: "Mercy of God"

Archangel Jeremiel is recognized by Eastern Orthodox tradition and in several noncanonical and Coptic books such as 2 Esdras, which outlines conversations between him and Ezra, and then later Zephaniah. Jeremiel explains that he watches over the departed souls from the great Flood.

In the Ethiopian Book of Enoch, Jeremiel is listed as one of the seven archangels and is frequently referred to as Ramiel. In this sacred text, as well as the noncanonical 2 Baruch, Jeremiel (Ramiel) is the angel of hope who inspires Divine visions and ministers to the souls who are set to ascend to Heaven.

With his ability to inspire spiritual visions, Jeremiel is a wonderful angel to summon when you're on a quest for inspiration. You can also call upon him to awaken your clairvoyance and dreams.

Life Reviews

Archangel Jeremiel is said to help newly crossed-over souls review their lives before they ascend to Heaven. He can also help those who ask to review their present life. In other words, you don't need to wait until your physical passage to have a life review. Archangel Jeremiel can be of assistance as you take inventory of your actions and adjust your future plans accordingly.

For example, Melanie Orders knew that she was meant to be a healer, but she felt unsure as to which direction to go. So she asked for guidance and drew a card from the *Archangel Oracle Cards* deck. The card

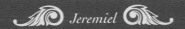

was the archangel Jeremiel, and he spoke of conducting a life review.

Melanie took this message to heart and decided to actually *do* this with the archangel's assistance. She went to a quiet, private place and meditated. Archangel Jeremiel came to her right away and took her on a life review, like watching a movie of her personal history.

First, Melanie experienced herself as a soul before birth, and she gained insight into why she made the decision to be born at this time. Next, she saw herself as a child who believed in fairies and who believed that she, too, could fly. She was shown her childhood friends and realized that they were all like little mermaids in their looks and demeanors.

Jeremiel showed Melanie all of her spiritual experiences and lessons that had occurred during childhood and adolescence, including the New Age books she'd written, the art classes she'd taken, and the yoga she'd done. He showed her how she'd always been attracted to massage and alternative health. With this life review, Melanie felt more clear and sure-footed about her path as a healer.

Jeremiel also helped protect Melanie and her family sometime later when a disgruntled ex-employee began leaving threatening messages on their answering machine and stalking them out of

revenge. Very frightened, Melanie asked the angels for assistance.

One evening as she was meditating, Melanie had a vision of a beautiful angel coming toward her. He seemed so calm, and he radiated great love. She instantly knew it was Archangel Jeremiel, who had helped her out of her confusion about her life's purpose. His patient, loving energy soothed her.

Jeremiel conveyed to Melanie that everything was going to work out fine. He said, "Just keep sending love to the man and his family; and to yourself, your husband, and your own family." Jeremiel asked Melanie to be strong and to release all worries and anger to him.

Every night Jeremiel appeared to Melanie, radiating light and asking her to visualize the situation as being resolved. About a week later, Melanie's father saw the ex-employee and confronted him about his behavior. The man apologized and said that he'd gotten a new job and was now happy. Since that time, he's left Melanie and her family alone.

Melanie feels so grateful to know that Jeremiel is available and willing to help her find patience, peace, and calmness.

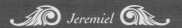
Jeremiel is a mentor and teacher who clearly guides us to see ourselves and others through the eyes of love. In the next chapter, we'll look at the archangel Zadkiel, who helps us remember our Divine heritage.

ZADKIEL

"Dear Archangel Zadkiel, thank you for helping me remember that I am a holy child of God."

Zadkiel is also known as: Sachiel, Tzadkiel, Zachariel, or Hesediel

Zadkiel's name means: "The righteousness of God"

Zadkiel is described in Jewish rabbinic writings as the archangel who inspires forgiveness and compassion in people. In the Kabbalah, Zadkiel (as Tzadkiel) presides over the fourth, or *Chesed*, Sephirah on the Tree of Life. The Chesed sphere relates to practicing unconditional kindness and love as a manifestation of God upon Earth.

Zadkiel is one of the seven archangels in the Gnostic tradition, as well as in the Pseudo-Dionysius writings. Under his alternative name Zachariel, he was identified as one of the seven archangels by Pope Saint Gregory.

Support for Students

"Dear Archangel Zadkiel, thank you for helping me recall all the necessary information that I need to know about this topic."

Zadkiel has long been regarded as the "angel of memory," who can support students and those who need to remember facts and figures.

For instance, when Celia Salazar didn't pass the exam to become a licensed professional engineer, she was devastated. As she prepped to retake the test, Celia found herself feeling nervous and unprepared. Fortunately, her sister Mary taught her about calling upon archangels Uriel (the angel of wisdom) and Zadkiel as study companions.

When it was time for Celia's second try at the exam, she asked for help and guidance from Uriel and Zadkiel. She noticed a ringing sound in her ears,

which she attributed to the archangels' presence and guidance. Celia also felt an indescribable sense of peace and confidence. Instead of taking eight hours, the exam only took her six.

The first time around, Celia had been left with a headache and tension. But with the help of Uriel and Zadkiel, on this occasion she felt filled with faith. And of course, she passed!

Healing Our Memories

"Thank you, Archangel Zadkiel, for helping me focus upon my beautiful memories and let the rest go."

Zadkiel's dual focus upon forgiveness and memory can help you heal emotional pain from your past. The archangel can work with you on releasing old anger or feelings of victimhood so that you can remember and live your Divine life purpose. As you ask Zadkiel for emotional healing, he'll shift your focus away from painful memories and toward the recollection of the beautiful moments of your life.

Linda Sue Blaylock loves connecting with Archangel Zadkiel, and she often receives profound messages from him during her meditations. Recently,

she wrote down some of those about connecting with other people:

> *Let down your guard, not only with yourself but with others. Now is the time for connections and love. Take notice of all the new souls entering your space now! Know that they are coming into your life for a specific reason, just as you are coming into theirs. Everyone has something to offer and share with another, including you! The uniqueness of each person is something to be appreciated and valued instead of judged. Look at your differences and celebrate the learning and sharing that can occur between you. You will be amazed by the new experiences and help that will be brought into your lives.*

Zadkiel counseled Linda Sue to keep an open mind with people from her past who reappeared in her life and not to judge. He advised her to heal old emotional wounds, promising, "The energetic shift will be immense; and the universe will blossom into a more peaceful, loving environment—a reality so many desire."

Archangel Zadkiel is a great healer of the mind, who gently leads you by the hand to take responsibility for your own happiness. In the Afterword, you'll meet additional archangels you may wish to call upon or work with.

AFTERWORD

OTHER NOTABLE ARCHANGELS

There are hundreds, perhaps thousands, of archangels in this universe. Ancient Jewish scripture says that each time God speaks, an angel is created. The vast majority of these angels and archangels are helpful, loving, trustworthy, and benevolent. If you wish to know whether to trust one, do research and rely on your body's reactions to the angel's name. If you feel relaxed and happy as you contemplate it, this is a good sign! If you ever have any uncomfortable feelings with a person, spirit, angel, or anyone else, then please heed this red flag and avoid that being in the future.

As this is a "101" (introductory) book on the archangel realm, I chose to focus on 15 of my favorites.

However, there are many others whom you may wish to explore and connect with, such as these time-honored and trustworthy archangels:

Barachiel, Baradiel, or Baraqiel: One of the seven archangels of Eastern Orthodox faith and named in the Book of Enoch, he protects against hailstorms, literal and metaphorical. Call upon Barachiel when you need strength to carry on.

Jegudiel or Jehudiel: This Gnostic and Eastern Orthodox archangel helps and supports those who are enduring trials or toiling for their Divine life mission. He protects and guides those who are devoted to working for the glory of God. In artwork, Jegudiel is portrayed holding a golden wreath.

Sealtiel or Selaphiel: This archangel is an intercessor of God who helps us stay focused upon our prayers so that we're praying from the heart without distraction. Sealtiel is one of the seven Gnostic archangels and is described in the third book of Esdras.

Tzaphkiel or Zaphkiel: This archangel presides over the *Binah* sphere of the Kabbalah's Tree of Life Sephiroth. Binah is the sacred feminine vessel of understanding and intuitive reasoning.

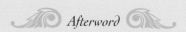
Zerachiel: One of the seven archangels named in the first book of Enoch, Zerachiel is an afterlife archangel who watches over abused children. His name means "God's command."

APPENDIX

SPECIALTIES OF THE ARCHANGELS

Michael—protection, courage, confidence, and safety; life-purpose guidance; fixing mechanical and electronic items.

Raphael—healing of people and animals; guiding healers in their education and practice; guidance and protection for travelers; connecting you with your soul mate.

Gabriel—delivering important and clear messages; helping those who are messengers (teachers, writers, actors, and artists); assisting with all aspects of parenting, including conception, adoption, and birth.

Uriel—intellectual understanding; conversations; ideas, insights, and epiphanies; studying, school, and test taking; writing and speaking.

Chamuel—universal and personal peace; finding whatever you are seeking.

Ariel—connecting with nature, animals, and nature spirits (for example, fairies); manifesting your earthly material needs; guidance for a career or avocation in environmentalism or animal welfare.

Metatron—sacred geometry and esoteric healing work; working with the universal energies, including time management and "time warping"; helping highly sensitive people (especially the youths who are often referred to as *Indigos* or *Crystals*).

Sandalphon—receiving and delivering prayers between God and humans; guidance and support for musicians.

Azrael—healing the bereaved; helping souls cross over; assisting grief counselors.

Jophiel—beautifying and uplifting your thoughts and feelings; clearing clutter out of your life.

Haniel—awakening and trusting your spiritual gifts of intuition and clairvoyance; releasing the old; support and healing for women's physical and emotional health issues.

Raziel—understanding the secrets of the universe; remembering and healing from past lives; understanding esoteric wisdom, such as dream interpretation.

Raguel—healing arguments or misunderstandings; bringing harmony to situations; attracting wonderful new friends.

Jeremiel—developing and understanding spiritual visions and clairvoyance; conducting a life review so you can make adjustments with respect to how you wish to live.

Zadkiel—helping students remember facts and figures for tests; healing painful memories; remembering your Divine spiritual origin and missions; choosing forgiveness.

Halo Colors
of the Archangels

Michael—royal purple, royal blue, and gold

Raphael—emerald green

Gabriel—copper

Uriel—yellow

Chamuel—pale green

Ariel—pale pink

Metatron—violet and green

Sandalphon—turquoise

Azrael—creamy white

Jophiel—dark pink

Haniel—pale blue (moonlight)

Raziel—rainbow colors

Raguel—pale blue

Jeremiel—dark purple

Zadkiel—deep indigo blue

CRYSTALS AND GEMSTONES ASSOCIATED WITH THE ARCHANGELS

Michael—sugilite

Raphael—emerald or malachite

Gabriel—copper

Uriel—amber

Chamuel—fluorite

Ariel—rose quartz

Metatron—watermelon tourmaline

Sandalphon—turquoise

Azrael—yellow calcite

Jophiel—rubellite or deep pink tourmaline

Haniel—moonstone

Raziel—clear quartz

Raguel—aquamarine

Jeremiel—amethyst

Zadkiel—lapis lazuli

ASTROLOGICAL SIGNS
ASSOCIATED WITH THE ARCHANGELS

Michael, Raphael, and Haniel—the overseers of all

Gabriel—*Cancer,* the nurturing and hardworking parent

Uriel—*Aquarius,* the thinker and analyzer

Chamuel—*Taurus,* the persistent finder of what is being sought

Ariel—*Aries,* the light, carefree, happy spirit

Metatron—*Virgo,* the hardworking, industrious, inventive, curious, serious perfectionist

Sandalphon—*Pisces,* the artsy dreamer

Azrael—*Capricorn,* the healer concerned with mortality and finality

Jophiel—*Libra,* the lover of beauty and orderliness

Raziel—*Leo,* the dramatic rainbow of colors and bright light

Raguel—*Sagittarius,* the sociable peacekeeper

Jeremiel—*Scorpio,* the truth teller who goes into shadows comfortably

Zadkiel—*Gemini,* the sociable but studious multitasker

ABOUT THE
AUTHOR

Doreen Virtue holds B.A. and M.A. degrees in counseling psychology from Chapman University, a Ph.D. in counseling psychology from California Coast University, and an associate's degree from Antelope Valley College. She is a lifelong clairvoyant who works with the angelic realm.

Doreen has previously written about archangels in her books *Healing with the Angels, How to Hear Your Angels, Messages from Your Angels, Archangels & Ascended Masters,* and *Solomon's Angels;* as well as the *Archangel Oracle Cards,* among other works. Her products are available in most languages worldwide.

Doreen has appeared on *Oprah,* CNN, *The View,* and other television and radio programs. She writes regular columns for *Woman's World, Spheres,* and *Spirit & Destiny* magazines. For more information on Doreen and the workshops she presents, please visit **www.AngelTherapy.com**.

You can listen to Doreen's live weekly radio show, and call her for a reading, by visiting **Hay HouseRadio.com**®.

Notes

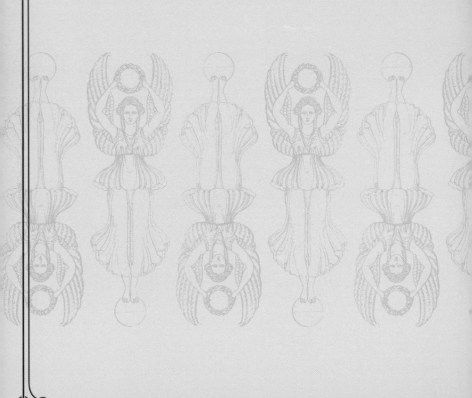

Notes

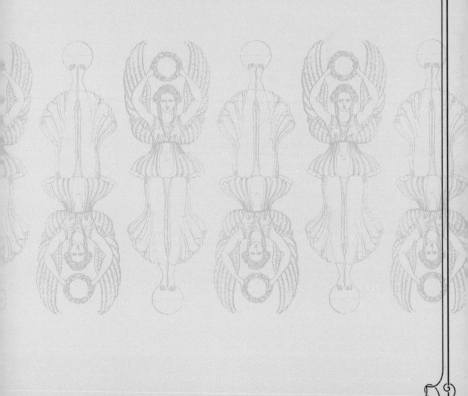

Notes

Notes

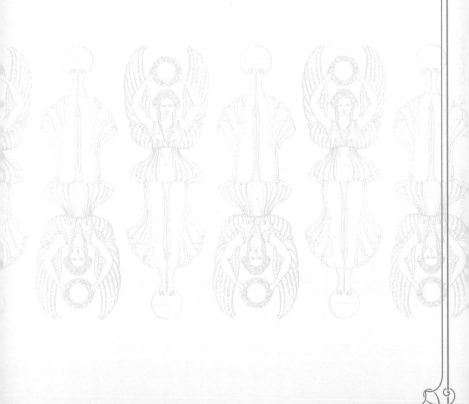

Notes

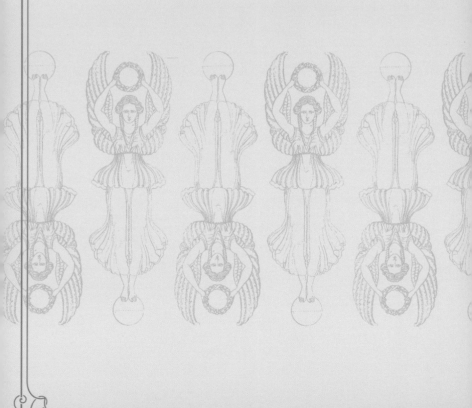

Notes

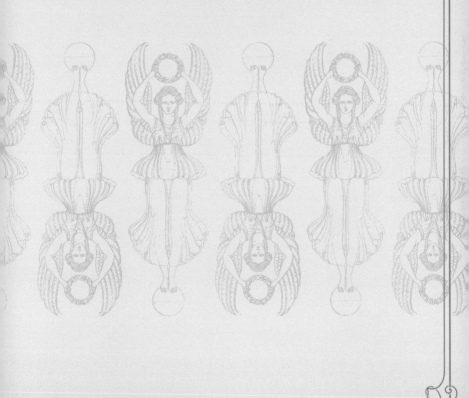

Hay House Titles of Related Interest

YOU CAN HEAL YOUR LIFE, the movie,
starring Louise L. Hay & Friends
(available as a 1-DVD program and an
expanded 2-DVD set) Watch the trailer at:
www.LouiseHayMovie.com

THE SHIFT, the movie,
starring Dr. Wayne W. Dyer (available as
a 1-DVD program and an expanded 2-DVD set)
Watch the trailer at: **www.DyerMovie.com**

⋏

*THE DIVINE NAME: The Sound That Can
Change the World,* by Jonathan Goldman

*LOVESCOPES: What Astrology Already Knows
about You and Your Loved Ones,* by Mark Husson

*MODERN-DAY MIRACLES: Miraculous Moments and
Extraordinary Stories from People All Over the World
Whose Lives Have Been Touched by Louise L. Hay,*
by Louise L. Hay & Friends

*OUR LADY OF KIBEHO: Mary Speaks to the World
from the Heart of Africa,* by Immaculée Ilibagiza

*THE SHIFT: Taking Your Life from Ambition
to Meaning,* by Dr. Wayne W. Dyer

TIME FOR TRUTH: A New Beginning, by Nick Bunick

TRAVELING AT THE SPEED OF LOVE,
by Sonia Choquette

*WRITING IN THE SAND: Jesus & the Soul of the
Gospels,* by Thomas Moore

All of the above are available at your local bookstore,
or may be ordered by contacting Hay House (see last page).

We hope you enjoyed this Hay House Lifestyles book. If you'd like to receive our online catalog featuring additional information on Hay House books and products, or if you'd like to find out more about the Hay Foundation, please contact:

Hay House, Inc., P.O. Box 5100, Carlsbad, CA 92018-5100
(760) 431-7695 or **(800) 654-5126**
(760) 431-6948 (fax) or **(800) 650-5115 (fax)**
www.hayhouse.com® • www.hayfoundation.org

Published and distributed in Australia by: Hay House
Australia Pty. Ltd., 18/36 Ralph St., Alexandria NSW 2015
Phone: 612-9669-4299 • *Fax:* 612-9669-4144
www.hayhouse.com.au

Published and distributed in the United Kingdom by:
Hay House UK, Ltd., 292B Kensal Rd., London W10 5B
Phone: 44-20-8962-1230 • *Fax:* 44-20-8962-1239
www.hayhouse.co.uk

Published and distributed in the Republic of South Africa by:
Hay House SA (Pty), Ltd., P.O. Box 990, Witkoppen 2068
Phone/Fax: 27-11-467-8904 • info@hayhouse.co.za
www.hayhouse.co.za

Published in India by: Hay House Publishers India, Muskaan
Complex, Plot No. 3, B-2, Vasant Kunj, New Delhi 110 070
Phone: 91-11-4176-1620 • *Fax:* 91-11-4176-1630
www.hayhouse.co.in

Distributed in Canada by: Raincoast, 9050 Shaughnessy St.,
Vancouver, B.C. V6P 6E5 • *Phone:* (604) 323-7100
Fax: (604) 323-2600 • www.raincoast.com

Take Your Soul on a Vacation

Visit **www.HealYourLife.com®** to regroup, recharge,
and reconnect with your own magnificence.
Featuring blogs, mind-body-spirit news, and life-
changing wisdom from Louise Hay and friends.

Visit **www.HealYourLife.com** today!